Christ Is Better—Don't Go Back

Embracing Grace in a Works World

Copyright © 2002

Dr. Larry Linkous

World rights reserved. No part of this publication may be stored in a retrieval system, transmitted, or reproduced in any way, including but not limited to photocopy, photograph, magnetic or other record, without prior agreement and written permission of the author.

Acknowledgements

To my savior Jesus Christ, who fills the deepest longings of my soul.

To my wife Sandra, a special word of deep appreciation and love, not only in relationship to this book, but in all my life and ministry. You are my beautiful and treasured covenant friend.

To my best male friend, my son Jason, my business partner and now my ministry partner as we "do all things for the sake of the Gospel." To his beautiful wife, Mindy and our two grandsons, Isaak and Elijah, such joys of our hearts.

To my parents, Bishop Malcolm and Hanna Linkous, for the deep treasure of Christian heritage you deposited in me and for all your love and prayers.

To Rita, my most trusted secretary. A woman of integrity and faith. You keep me reminded. To Sheri and Gretchen, and all the girls who helped so much.

To a great staff of pastors, secretaries, and workers who believe in us.

To the greatest family of believers in the world who make up New Life Christian Fellowship. I am so honored to be your pastor.

To Dr. Ronald E. Cottle for helping make this happen.

To my mentor, Dr. Roy Harthern.

To my pastor, Dr. Houston Miles.

To everyone who has brought me correction, love, and prayer. You have touched and guided my life.

To each one who takes the time to read and understand.

May God bless you abundantly.

Table of Contents

Preface 7

Introduction 9

Chapter 1—**Christ Is Better** 15

Chapter 2—**Relationships, Not Religion** 33

Chapter 3—**Christ Brings a Better Faith** 51

Chapter 4—**Is It Legal to Be Free of the Law?** 65

Chapter 5—**Salvation, God's Gift to You** 87

Chapter 6—**It's Really Very Simple** 103

Chapter 7—**Don't Go Back!** 119

Preface

"Everyone tells me what a joy it is to follow Jesus, but it's really hard for me," moaned a frustrated listener to my radio program. That confession rings true for millions of churchgoers and religious folks. Perhaps it's true for you.

- Ever feel really tired of being a Christian?
- Do you struggle with all the don'ts while rarely having the energy left to do the do's?
- Have you ever found your mind wandering aimlessly in church while the preacher preached or everyone else was singing but your life seemed aimless instead of focused?
- Do you have a boring Christian life while those you watch on TV or listen to seem to have lives overflowing with faith, hope, grace and miracles?
- Is the Bible more of a rule book for you than a guide to joyful living?
- Do you find yourself wishing you had great faith but wondering why you doubt so much?
- Is Christianity just part of your life, or does it fill your life with meaning and purpose?
- Are you learning more and more about Christ but lack an intimate relationship with him?

If you've ever asked these questions, I have exciting answers for you. Your religious existence is about to be transformed into a dynamic relationship with Jesus Christ.

In reading this book, you will discover that Christ is better than…

- Religious ritual
- Law and rules
- Past traditions
- Church membership
- Doing the right thing but never living an abundant life

After reading this book, you will never go back to the old baggage of your past or of the dull religion that you've been carrying around. It's time for God's grace to set you free and to take you to a new level of excitement about Christ.

Weary of the old stuff? Good. You're about to discover that **Christ is better!**

Introduction

"...regulations...imposed until the time of reformation."
                                    (Hebrews 9:10 NASB)

The Book of Hebrews, like no other New Testament Epistle, is a book of reformation. Hebrews burns bridges. It neither embraces the past, nor appeases the past. The message of Hebrews picks up where the Epistles of Paul finish. Without apology or timidity, the author of Hebrews embraces and proclaims the power of the New Covenant. Rejected is any idea of first covenant validity in relationship to the New Testament believer's salvation and continuing maturity.

The loud and irrevocable message of Hebrews is: **Christ is better!**

According to Hebrews, Christ is better and everything that has preceded Him in the first covenant was just a shadow of the Good Thing to come—Jesus Christ Himself. Therefore, all unnecessary baggage must be abandoned, discarded, and left behind. To carry it along into the new life found in Christ alone is to fail to lay aside every weight and sin that invite strife and stumbling, thus entangling the Christian life with the works of old covenant law.

Cumbersome religious irrelevance is stripped away from both the believer and the corporate church when the book of Hebrews is understood and interpreted using the proper keys and historical background. This establishes an exegetical system that allows the powerful message of the slain and resurrected Christ to be revealed and released to a lost and dying world.

Hebrew's message is **relevance.** The writer has no choice. He can't look back because this is an emergency. His letter urgently appeals to a group of Hebrews in the first century New Testament church who have heard the Good News preached to them but have not mixed what they have heard with faith in Christ. That faith allows the salvation process to be completed in their hearts. They're in trouble in this precarious, incomplete condition and are experiencing extreme persecution, having been identified with the true believers in the church. Because of their incompleteness, now amplified by unbearable persecution, they are leaning toward retreating to and relying upon the temple rituals of animal blood and ceremonial traditions of the old law. To go back would destroy every opportunity for completed salvation and sever them from any hope of a true and complete relationship in Christ.

Hebrews may or may not have been written by Paul. That argument is reserved for the scholars. If it were, then it was written from a different perspective than any of his other New Testament letters. Hebrews does not reach back and attempt to appease the Jews and their Old Covenant tradition.

Paul, being the champion of the revelation of grace, is careful to reach to his "brethren" in an attempt to entice them or at the least not offend them while he himself remains true to the gospel. However, Hebrews loses all of that finesse. While not deliberately offensive, Hebrews moves forthrightly to the heart of the New Testament message that Jesus Christ is better. He is better than Moses, better than angels, better than Aaron. Jesus Christ brings a better blood, a better sacrifice, a better tabernacle, a better faith, etc. Jesus Christ is better and is the fulfillment of all that the first covenant foreshadowed. There is no reason, no cause, no salvation, and no hope in reaching back to works of the Law and first testament blood. To do so would trample under foot the Son of God, and regard the blood of His covenant unclean, thus insulting the Spirit of Grace (Hebrews 10:29).

If Paul did not write this Epistle, then it was most necessarily written by one of his disciples, a son in the faith. He would have been a first generation disciple absent of any perceived need to pacify the old Hebrew religion of first covenant blood and ceremony.

Whoever wrote it demanded a reformation that called to the church then and continues to call today. This call was for the New Testament church to refuse the yoke of old law burdens and first covenant ceremonialism, and get on with the relevant message of grace brought and bought by Jesus Christ. This same message of grace was revealed to and through Paul in his thirteen Epistles in the New Testament. This was a call for the church to strip off all the irrelevance of religion and move to the heart of the New Covenant gospel; redemption through Christ's blood and His blood alone.

Regarding the Old Testament Scriptures

Because of the nature of the subject matter in this book, some may question how I feel about the Old Testament Scriptures. I must, therefore, express my love and acceptance of the treasure of great truth and revelation contained in the pages of the Old Testament.

The Bible teaches us to cling to the New Testament as our avenue of salvation, righteousness, and maturity and refuse to embrace the Levitical system and the works of the Old Testament Law. However, the Bible by no means teaches us to reject the treasures of the Old Testament Scriptures that enrich our lives and enhance our spiritual understanding. Consider the stories of these great men: Noah, Abraham, Joseph, Moses, David, Isaac, Jonah, Isaiah, Jeremiah, and Daniel. Consider the stories of battles and victories, lessons of life, and the types and shadows of the coming Messiah—Jesus Christ. Read the prophecies of Israel, the Christ, end times, and the endless list of truths and treasures in the Old Testament Scriptures.

We would lose a great heritage of faith if we in any way discarded or discredited any of these jewels in our overview of the Bible and our understanding of God. Therefore, we will enjoy the Old Testament, preach from it, and learn from it. We will take from it all that is pointed to in Jesus Christ and the fulfillment of all things in Him. <u>Refusing to live under the Law and its curse does not discard the Old Testament Scripture as part of the Bible.</u>

I believe the account of creation in Genesis. I believe there was a great flood in the days of Noah and that God used water to destroy the world to preserve His bloodline in Noah. I learn rich truths from the life of Joseph and how humility promoted him to a place of high honor. I thrill at the deliverance of Israel from Pharaoh and Egypt and learn great truths for my own life and ministry from their refusal to go into the Promised Land. I'm amazed at the clear picture of the Christ in Leviticus and the continuing revelation of the Messiah throughout the Old Testament as it unfolds toward His revealed life in the New Testament. I love to study David the musician and warrior; Nehemiah, the builder of the wall and restorer of worship; Isaiah, Elijah, Elisha, and Jeremiah; Ezekiel and the valley of dry bones (Israel).

We have a treasure chest of truths and prophecy in the Old Testament Scriptures that points toward the coming Messiah and encourages us in many ways. However, the focus of the subject matter of this book concerns other matters, not these topics. Nevertheless, one must always recognize Old Testament

Scripture as anointed and Holy Spirit inspired.

> *All Scripture is inspired by God and profitable for teaching, for reproof, for correction, for training in righteousness; that the man of God may be adequate, equipped for every good work.*
>
> (2 Timothy 3:16-17 NASB)

Chapter 1

Christ Is Better

Both my grandfathers retired from the coal mines of West Virginia near Charleston. I'll never forget my childhood memories of my grandfather Linkous, black from the coal dust that clung to him when he came home from his shift in the #9 mine in Cabin Creek hollow.

A few years ago, we all went back—my mom and dad, my brother and his wife, my wife Sandra and me. It had been forty years since I left and this was my first time back. It's strange how the memories flooded over me, and even more strange how they stirred emotions that seemed to churn just below the surface.

But it wasn't like I remembered it. Things had changed as time passed, and now all that was left were my memories.

You Can't Go Back

Have you ever tried to go back where you grew up? Back to the old neighborhood, the farmhouse, the schoolyard? There are some pretty mixed emotions back there, but the most emphatic lesson you learn about going back is that you can't go back! If any amount of time has passed, it's just not the same.

Memories have deceived you. The schoolhouse, once so large now seems small. The homestead has been torn down and the corner store is an attorney's office. The gas station is abandoned and the windows are knocked out, and by the price on the worn sign (Gas .49$\underline{9}$) you know about when the last people tried to make the station a success.

Furthermore, if the places stayed the same, the people hadn't. The Bailey family moved away, as did so many of your old friends. The refinery closed down and people had to go elsewhere for jobs. Mrs. Johnson is a widow. She thinks she remembers you, but she doesn't see very well anymore and her memory isn't like it used to be.

Remember that good-looking boyfriend with the dark hair and muscles you bragged about? Well, he's the one guy you wished you wouldn't have found. He's waiting tables at the diner, and what were once muscles now droop around his waist, and his hair has dropped completely away! It's amazing how nice your husband looks all of a sudden!

When the going gets rough our minds often tend to take us back to easier days. We dream of the good 'ole days when things weren't so intense, busy, and stressed. Back then, life seemed slower, kinder and gentler. Maybe, but going back is only a figment of our imagination, no matter how good it seems for the moment.

Nevertheless, you're here now. Life has changed and things have changed, but more important, you have changed. None of that stuff back there would work for you or fulfill you even if it were the same because you're different now. It's a different day and you're a different person, and a better person for it.

Though imagination and memories of the past may be a place to rest for a moment, it's no place to live. You don't fit there anymore than it fits you.

We Are Created to Grow

We weren't created to go back, we were created to grow. God is always doing a new thing, birthing new ideas and moving us forward into truth and new revelation. Our God is a God of new beginnings, fresh starts, and forward vision. He leads us forward the same as He leads society and the church to a new world in Him and around Him.

God has given us many Holy Spirit empowered change agents to get us where He wants us to be. God has a great plan to move us forward even farther than our fleshly mind could imagine. Let's not listen to the voices that beckon us to go back. There's nothing back there for us. We're new creations because God has changed us.

Join with me to discover new and exciting dimensions of God's promises and God's power. Let's explore some vital new truths from God's word that will impact our lives in a most dramatic way. Let's look at the revelation of Hebrews as it speaks to us from a bygone age with truth of an eternal nature that never grows old or outdated.

Jesus Christ—The Revelation of Hebrews

Just as in our earthly life, there can be no healthy value in remaining in our past, so it is true in our spiritual life. Constantly looking back does not create the proper environment for maturity and spiritual growth. To the recipients of the letter to the Hebrews, refusing to let go of the past and reach forward to the promise offered them meant losing the opportunity of eternal life in Christ. This is why the message of Hebrews is such a vital truth regarding our New Testament theology and our right standing in Christ. Although this book is not necessarily designed as a study of Hebrews, a proper understanding of it will help us discover the value in reaching forward to what lies ahead.

The book of Hebrews is not an easy read. Nevertheless, it is full of vital truth and valuable Bible doctrine pertinent to the church and Christian life. Hebrews is an Epistle, a letter written to the early church either by the apostle Paul or an unknown author. It opens by proclaiming the foremost important doctrine of the New Testament—the deity of Christ.

> *"He* [Jesus Christ] *is the radiance of His* [God's] *glory and the exact representation of His nature, and upholds all things by the word of His power. When He had made purification of sins, He sat down at the*

right hand of the Majesty on high."

Hebrews 1:3

This powerful statement of truth is the single most vital plank in the foundation of the Church. No doctrine is more important; it sets the value of Hebrews to the New Testament church.

We must be committed to understanding the book of Hebrews both for the truth it brought the first century Hebrews and for the light it sheds on the rest of the Word of God throughout each generation. Though it can be difficult, Hebrews must not be isolated from the rest of the Bible lest we lose valuable revelational and anointed insight.

The most valuable truth that emerges from Hebrews is God's commitment to us through Jesus Christ. God shed forth His grace through the person of His Son and showed us that we must receive from Him by grace what we can't earn for ourselves—salvation.

Grace is the engine that moves us through life and brings us on the other side. We stand in God's presence, not because we are holy in and of ourselves, but because He showers us with His grace through Jesus, the Anointed One.

Use the Instruments

There can be no proper exegetical understanding of the Hebrews without having a firm grasp on its historical background.

> *Analysis and historical background is to the Bible student desirous of truth what a compass is to a mariner or a radar screen is to an aviator. There is no reaching the destination without the aid of their*

> *instruments. **The expositor of Hebrews cannot hope to arrive at a correct understanding of the truth (exegesis) of this book without constantly checking his position by its historical background or analysis.*** (*Wuest's Volume II Word Studies in the Greek New Testament*, p.13)

It is evident by the title that this letter to the Hebrews was written to one of the first New Testament churches consisting primarily of Jews. Furthermore, the existence of the temple and practice of animal sacrifices mentioned throughout the text is evidence that this church existed prior to the destruction of Jerusalem in 70 AD. The importance of this historical data becomes clear as the text progresses. Though the letter is addressed to the Hebrews, don't underestimate its value and necessity to the entire church, whether Jew or Gentile. This epistle lives and pertains vitally to the entire Body of Christ today!

Two major themes surface and grab the reader's attention throughout this letter.

Theme #1: Christ Is better.

This theme is readily noticed with just a surface summary of Hebrews. The key word is "better" and the over riding message is ***Christ Is Better***. This theme is key to the message of the Epistle.

> 1:4 *"having become as much **better** than the angels, as He has inherited a more excellent name than they."*

> 6:9 *"But, beloved, we are convinced of **better** things concerning you, and things that accompany salvation, though we are speaking in this way."*

7:7 *"But without any dispute the lesser is blessed by the greater."* better blessing

7:19 *"(for the Law made nothing perfect), and on the other hand there is a **better** hope, through which we draw near to God."*

8:6 *"But now He has obtained a **more excellent** ministry, but as much as He is also the mediator of a **better** covenant, which has been enacted on **better** promises."*

9:23 *"Therefore it was necessary for the copies of things in the heavens to be cleansed with these, but the heavenly things themselves with **better** sacrifices than these."*

10:34 *"For you showed sympathy to the prisoners, and accepted joyfully the seizure of your property, knowing that you have for yourselves a **better** possession and an abiding one."*

11:16 *"But as it is, they desire a **better** country, that is a heavenly one. Therefore God is not ashamed to be called their God; for He has prepared a city for them."*

11:35 *"Women received back their dead by resurrection; and others were tortured, not accepting their release, in order that they might obtain a **better** resurrection."*

11:40 *"because God had provided something **better** for us, so that apart from us they should not be made perfect."*

Christ is better than…

- Angels
- Moses

- Aaron
- Melchizedek
- Abraham
- Isaac
- Jacob
- everyone else listed in Hebrews and the entire Bible narrative

Christ offers a better…
- Blood
- Covenant
- Sacrifice
- Tabernacle
- Priesthood
- Hope
- Salvation
- Faith

The narrative of Hebrews is clear: ***Christ is better***!

Theme #2: Don't go back.

This second theme is not written in the letter, but it is clearly perceived in every line of every verse. This theme is—Don't Go Back!

For this statement to be meaningful, we must examine the condition of this local church at the time the letter was written. Two factors are at once evident, and each brought its own characteristics.

1. Persecution

Persecution was pressing upon this Hebrew Christian church unlike any they had ever experienced. They were not only cast out of their families and out of the temple, but now their property and even their very existence were being threatened. This church and these people were under extreme persecution *"from apostate Judaism in an effort to force them to renounce their professed faith in Messiah and return to the First Testament sacrifices"* (Wuest p.73).

2. Refining Fire

This young church was thrust into the forge of persecution and bathed in the heat of honed fire. They learned that suffering persecution defined their beliefs and refined their faith. They had to decide early on whether or not their belief in Christ was worthy of persecution. When faced with persecution, and in this case extreme persecution including grave harm or even death, all our belief systems come under scrutiny. James 1:12 said *"Blessed is a man who perseveres under trial; for once he has been approved, he will receive the crown of life which the Lord has promised to those who love Him."* Persecution will cause us to examine our belief system.

Leave the Baggage

Something about suffering persecution refines and defines you. You will not suffer for what you don't believe. If you've ever suffered for your testimony, your principles, or the stand you've taken on any issue, you decide something early on. You decide whether you truly believe in what you're suffering for or if you're suffering for a belief you've adopted from someone else. When the attack begins, you come to a clear-cut decision about where you stand on any issue. You'll suffer for what you really believe, and possibly even die for it. However, if you don't believe it or if you've borrowed it without thorough examination, you'll discard it right away. You won't suffer for what you don't believe. There's no need to, so why should you?

A good thing about suffering is that it refines you and in a real sense defines you. You emerge from a trial more streamlined than when you went in. During the trial, you discover what baggage you've picked up, and what baggage is unnecessary that you don't really believe. These beliefs have been hindering your progress all along but it took suffering to identify them. This heavy struggle wears you out, weighs you down, and beats you up until you realize how unnecessary it is and you cast it away from yourself.

Cut it loose and cast it aside. You're in a battle and that extra weight is costing you valuable victories. It weighs you down and is boiling you over. Hebrews 12:1 declares,

> *Therefore, since we have so great a cloud of witnesses surrounding us, let us also lay aside every encumbrance, and the sin which so easily entangles us, and let us run with endurance the race that is set before us.*

As a young child, I was traveling with my parents across the Great Smokey Mountains in Tennessee. These were the largest mountains I had ever seen and seemed to me to be the biggest mountains in the world. I remember how slow our car was winding up the steep grades of the Smokey Mountain roadway. Semi-trucks grinding up the hills pulling their heavy loads would often slow us even more. I remember seeing one truck that was moving so slowly the driver opened his door and was standing on the running board while the truck crept up the hill.

Other trucks were stopped along the side of the highway with radiators boiling over and spouting steam from the intense temperature.

This graphic memory reminds me of many Christians. They become weary dragging so much unnecessary baggage through their lives. They carry heavy loads of jealousy, judgment, insecurity, fear, and strife, or loads of painful wounds from abuse. Travel would be so much easier if they could lay aside what they're dragging in their lives and be set free from their burdens. Too many Christians are sitting along the roadside as life passes them by, boiling over from the heat and weight of their load.

Lay aside every weight so that you can testify like Peter *"that the proof of your faith, being more precious than gold which is perishable, even though tested by fire, may be found to result in praise and glory and honor at the revelation of Jesus Christ"* (1 Peter 1:7).

On the other side of suffering you have defined what you believe. You have shed the load. Now, you're a prepared warrior, ready to overcome every attack of the enemy.

Two Kinds of People

This intense cauldron of suffering in the Hebrew church caused them to define what they really believed. This church, as in most every church in the world, had two kinds of people:

- True Christians who accept and follow Jesus Christ. This group had heard the gospel message of salvation through Christ's blood, mixed the message with faith (Hebrews 4:2), and received Christ into their hearts as Savior (Romans 10:9-10). They were truly Christians.

- Those who know about the Gospel but have not received Jesus Christ into their hearts. This group had heard the Good News preached to them. They had mentally assented to the Gospel and possibly had identified outwardly through water baptism, but had not received Christ into their hearts as Savior. For these people, salvation was incomplete; they were lost in their sin. The salvation process had not come full circle for them and in them. Thus, they were outside the circle of true believers.

Until the persecution began, the second group probably seemed just like the true Christians. They sang the songs, faithfully attended, worked around the church, cut the grass, baked the cookies, and possibly even gave their money. Nevertheless, they were lost. Hebrews 4:2 says,

> *For indeed we have had good news preached to us, just as they also; but the word they heard did not profit them, because it was not united by faith in those who heard.*

What a tragedy. Many people will miss heaven by just the distance between their head and their heart. You don't receive Christ through osmosis. Hanging around Christians will not ensure your personal salvation. Your grandfather may have been a great preacher. Your dad may have been the head deacon. Or your mom may be the most godly person you know, but you still must receive Christ for yourself. No one else can stand in for you in regard to your personal salvation. Jesus Christ is knocking at *your* door and only *you* can open it.

There Is None Good but God

People often mistake the good behavior of others as an attribute of goodness within them. However, this can be no farther from truth. Without Christ, there is no goodness in us. Yes, we may appear to be moral creatures, but the truth is we are at enmity with God and are enemies of the cross. Comments about others such as, "they're such good people"; "they're great folks"; they're such nice neighbors; they haven't received Christ, but they're so good" imply that simply being good is enough.

We know what they mean, and we do appreciate neighbors who aren't cursing and shooting at us. Nevertheless, in the eyes of God, they're not good. We have our religious list of good and bad and our list of who's in and who's out. We even have a list of the top ten worst sins, and though not necessarily in the same order, most of our lists contain the same sins:

1. Murder
2. Adultery
3. Homosexuality
4. Abortion
5. Abuse
6. Alcoholism
7. Drug Addiction
8. Lying
9. Stealing
10. Cheating

Rearrange the list any way you desire. Take some things off and add your own. It doesn't matter to God, because the most grievous sin of all isn't on that list.

Rebellion—The Road to Destruction

To God, the most detestable sin in the world is refusing to bow to Him and call Him Lord. It's the sin of *Rebellion*. This is the sin Cain committed which ultimately moved him to kill his brother. Its humanism at its finest (or its worst). Rebellion means not doing things God's way. Cain liked what was produced by the labor of his own hands but wouldn't humble himself to provide the blood of a little lamb.

The rebellious lie of the humanistic New Age is that it's good enough. It says, *"God is in all of us and if we dig deep enough, improve enough, and meditate enough we really don't need this blood of Jesus stuff."*

The rebellious self-sufficiency of man declares that he really doesn't need a savior; he can handle things himself. This is the vilest sin in the universe. This sin disregards the love of God and the blood covenant gift that Jesus Christ poured out from His veins while hanging between two thieves on the gory cross of Calvary. God hates and resists that sin. A "good" person, depending on his own goodness, is light years farther away from God than the HIV-positive, drug-addicted prostitute who falls on her face in the puddle of her own failures and cries out for a savior!

Jesus tells of the Pharisee in Luke 18:9-14:

> *And He also told this parable to certain ones who trusted in themselves that they were righteous, and viewed others with contempt: "Two men went up into the temple to pray, one a Pharisee, and the other a tax-gatherer. The Pharisee stood and was praying thus to himself, 'God, I thank Thee that I am not like other people: swindlers, unjust, adulterers, or even like this tax-gatherer. I fast twice a week; I pay tithes all of that I get.' But the tax-gatherer, standing some*

distance away, was even unwilling to lift up his eyes to heaven, but was beating his breast, saying, 'God, be merciful to me, the sinner!' I tell you, this man went down to his house justified rather than the other; for everyone who exalts himself shall be humbled, but he who humbles himself shall be exalted."

Christ Is Better—Don't Go Back

The Hebrews's church had in attendance a population of mentally assenting people. They had not received Christ in their hearts and so were leaning back toward the animal sacrifices of the Law. Therefore, the author of this Epistle primarily addressed this group. These individuals were in crisis.

A key Bible interpretation principle must be applied to every verse and chapter to properly understand this Epistle. We must use these two fundamental and vitally necessary keys:

- Christ Is Better
- Don't Go Back

Along with understanding the historical background of this church, these two keys unlock the awesome beauty and deep doctrinal revelation of Hebrews.

Now that Christ has come, don't go back to something far more inferior. Because Christ is better, don't go back to

- temple worship
- the Levitical system
- works of the Law
- the Aaronic priesthood

- the blood of bulls and goats and doves

Colossians 2:13-17 states:

> *And when you were dead in your transgressions and the uncircumcision of your flesh, He made you alive together with Him, having forgiven us all our transgressions, having canceled out the certificate of debt consisting of decrees against us and which was hostile to us; and He has taken it out of the way, having nailed it to the cross. When He had disarmed the rulers and authorities, He made a public display of them, having triumphed over them through Him. Therefore let no one act as your judge in regard to food or drink or in respect to a festival or a new moon or a Sabbath day—things which are a mere shadow of what is to come; but the substance of what belongs to Christ.*

Keep feeding the faith that has started working in you and come full circle to not only assenting in your mind to Him as a good person, but to fully accepting Christ in your heart as Savior as well.

Remember these Key Points:

1. **You Can't Go Back**

    Yesterday's news is just that—yesterday's news. You can't recapture your youthful memories and think things will be the same. You've grown too much.

2. **You Are Created to Grow**

    You are a living being and to remain alive, you must grow. As we grow in relationship with Jesus, His life becomes an integral part of ours.

3. **Jesus Christ—The Revelation of Hebrews**

    The primary revelation of the letter to the Hebrews is the grace of God made real through Jesus Christ. Jesus is the central focus of the Epistle, and His supremacy is the main theme.

4. **Use the Instruments**

    To understand the Book of Hebrews, you must use the instruments provided. Any other tool will fall short of correct exegesis. These tools include understanding the historical background and proper analysis of the context.

5. **Leave the Baggage**

    Everyone has baggage in their lives. It's heavy, cumbersome, and usually filled with junk. Get rid of it!

6. **Two Kinds of People**

    There are Christians for whom Christ is Savior, and people who are Christians in name only. The latter have mentally assented to Him, but He's not in their hearts.

7. **There Is None Good but God**

    No matter how hard you try, you can't earn your salvation by your own goodness. Everyone has sinned and has fallen short of God's glory (Rom 3:23), so what makes you think you are any different?

8. **Rebellion—The Road to Destruction**

    Rebellion is the vilest sin of all. It implies that one doesn't need God, nor would one accept Him even if he did. Rebellion is closely akin to idolatry because of the focus of worship.

9. **Christ Is Better—Don't Go Back**

Many attending the first church in Hebrews were in danger. They had only mentally assented to the Gospel but had not come full circle and received Christ in their hearts as Savior and King. Now under heavy persecution, they were leaning back to temple ritual and animal blood. To do so would sever them from Christ.

Chapter 2

Relationships, Not Religion

A bright, sunlit sky greeted Collin as he stepped out of the door of the Salvation Army and merged into the throng of busy people at the downtown crosswalk. Once away from the Salvation Army, you wouldn't have noticed the difference between him and anyone else on the street that day. He had showered and shaved, and had put on the new clothes the Salvation Army had given him, clothes that fit surprisingly well. Other than being a bit thin, he could have been any successful family man out for a casual time of shopping. But he wasn't.

Collin was a professional panhandler—a transient—and just a few blocks away he began to ply his trade. First he approached a shopper and then a businessman, trying to gather up enough treasure to purchase some cigarettes. Ultimately, if he were lucky, he'd get enough to buy that cheap bottle of heaven that would get him through one more day.

Collin was grown, an adult, and for the most part looked pretty much like any other guy in town that morning. But even though grown and adult, he was far from whole, and by evening, if he succeeded, he would be staggering and searching for a park bench on which to make a bed. He was a street person, having known this style of living most of his life.

Collin couldn't hold down a regular nine-to-five job. In fact, he couldn't hold down any job. Something in his emotional makeup seemed to prevent that kind of commitment. He couldn't be boxed in because it smothered him. He had to wander and pander and move on. Collin couldn't trust and couldn't be trusted.

It would be interesting to study Collin's life—his childhood, adolescence, being passed around from uncle to cousin to friend to orphanage. Growing older all the time, looking the adult part but ultimately living on the streets with not only holes in his soles, but a great big hole in his soul as well.

Security Leads to Maturity

Security fosters growth into maturity. Conversely, the lack of security inhibits growth and results in chronic immaturity. One can grow older in Christ without necessarily growing up in Him. Growing up in Christ depends on one's relationship with Him and how it is perceived.

Growing into maturity is part of God's purpose in your life. Paul addressed this with the church in Ephesus, and how growing to maturity results in a strong faith not easily swayed or turned:

And He Himself gave some to be apostles, some prophets, some evangelists, and some pastors and teachers, for the equipping of the saints for the work of ministry, for the edifying of the body of Christ, **till** *we all come to the unity of the faith and of the knowledge of the Son of God, to a perfect man, to the measure of the stature of the fullness of Christ; that we should no longer be children, tossed to and fro and carried about with every wind of doctrine, by the trickery of men, in the cunning craftiness of deceitful plotting, but, speaking the truth in love, may grow up in all things into Him who is the head—Christ...*

(Ephesians 4:11-15 NKJV)

Religion vs. Relationship

From cover to cover, the Bible is about relationships. The primary concern is not with religion but with relationships. The Bible clearly indicates that God desires a relationship with His human creation (that's you). He wants more than to only be Creator, God, Boss, Lord, or Bishop. God longs for a close, personal relationship with you. He yearns to be your friend.

Because of that desire Christ came to earth, born of a virgin impregnated by the seed of God, wrapped in a robe of flesh, and announced by angels. Christ Jesus came and lived among His creation for thirty-three years. He ate our food, worked our jobs, sweated our sweat, cried our tears, shared our laughter and ultimately died our death.

Jesus is God and man all in the same instance, hanging between two thieves on a gory cross reserved for felons, pouring out the blood of God that redeemed humankind from sin. All of this so He could have a relationship with you! Now, He stands at the door and knocks (Rev. 3:12), and if you will open the door, He will come in and fellowship. Jesus Christ died for the opportunity to have a relationship with you.

You must realize and appreciate this important fact before you can enjoy a relationship with Him. Otherwise you will be driven by fear and insecurity. Then, every time you sin or fail or trespass you will be afraid and will turn to run away from the One who begs you to run to Him (Hebrews 4: 14-16).

We've been lied to about God. Some people have a false picture in their mind of a God that is just waiting for them to slip so He can beat them with His club.

If God had wanted you to writhe in pain and be afraid of Him, he would never have left the glory-flashing rainbow encircled throne of God. He would have remained seated, and would have watched you suffer from that high and lofty position.

However, God stood up, dressed Himself in a robe of flesh and entered your world to purchase you back to Himself. Jesus relinquished His form of God and set it aside to come in the form of a man (Philippians 2:6-7). That's redemption. God isn't mad at you. God loves you. He even likes you. He delights over you according to Psalms 18:19, and desires your intimacy. When you believe that, your love for Him will grow, and you will want to be around Him. In fact, you'll run to Him. This security will lead you to maturity.

Street Smart

Like Collin, people who grow up on the streets become what we call "street smart." Often, these people were passed around from uncles to grandparents to foster homes or anywhere they could find a bed and shelter. They became tough and learned to survive under very difficult circumstances. When you look at them they look as normal as anyone else, but because of their upbringing, they lack security. They have big holes in their emotional make up. They find it difficult to trust because their outlook and their commitment is bruised and slanted by the way they were raised. Unless they are healed emotionally, their lives will be negatively impacted by their upbringing. They may be fully grown, but because of their insecurity they have maturity issues—holes in their souls.

It's no different with Christians. If we can't trust the Father, if we can't run to Him and rest in His love and care, we have problems. We may grow older in Christ, but big holes exist in our trust, faith, security, and maturity.

If you've been raised fearing that God is going to abandon you every time you falter, fail, or sin, then your view of God is twisted and tainted from your past experience. You're unhealthy spiritually because you're insecure in God's covenant of love for you. God will never leave you, nor forsake you. You can do nothing to make Him love you more than He does right now, and you can do nothing to make Him love you less. He is not human, so He doesn't act or react out of wounded human emotions. God has decided to love you, embrace you, and cover you, and His covenant heart will never change. Once you comprehend this, you will relax into His love and His eternal care. Your security will result in maturity.

> *Since then we have a great high priest who has passed through the heavens, Jesus the Son of God, let us hold fast our confession. For we do not have a high priest who cannot sympathize with our weaknesses, but one who has been tempted in all things as we are, yet without sin. Let us therefore draw near with confidence to the throne of grace, that we may receive mercy and may find grace to help in time of need.*
>
> (Hebrews 4:14-16)

Great comfort can be yours because God came to earth in the

form of a man. He took the name of Jesus, lived a pure and holy life without sin, gave Himself up to be brutally killed for your sin, was raised from the dead, and is now seated at the right hand of God interceding for you. How much more beautiful a story can be told than that of the mighty love of God for you?

Jesus told the incredible story of the Prodigal Son in Luke 15:11-32. However, I think the name of the story puts the emphasis in the wrong place. It is much more the story of a loving father who waits patiently for his son to return to him and find rest. I challenge you to read it again and discover something new.

A Scary Thought

To misunderstand the epistle of Hebrews is to embrace false teaching, believe wrongly, and become confused in areas concerning your relationship with Christ and your security in Him. Hebrews can be "intimidating" without proper interpretation.

Come with me now back to Hebrews and allow me to use a verse to exemplify how vital a proper interpretation of Hebrews is to your security in Christ: *"For if we go on sinning willfully after receiving the knowledge of the truth, there no longer remains a sacrifice for sins"* (Hebrews 10:26). That's a scary statement! On the surface, this verse says that if one sins after receiving Christ there is no hope for salvation and a sacrifice no longer remains for them.

The good news is that it isn't true! That is not a proper rendering of this Scripture. To understand this verse we must apply our two keys of interpretation: **Christ Is Better** and **Don't Go Back**. Only by using these keys will we unlock the truth to this verse.

Under the light of our keys, we see that this verse is an appeal to first century Hebrews who have only mentally assented to the Gospel not to go back. Going back to the temple sacrifices, the Law works of the Old Covenant and the dead ceremonialism of the Levitical system would be a most tragic and grievous sin.

After understanding the work of Christ on Calvary and why his blood was poured (not the blood of bulls and goats), to go back to trusting in animal blood would be a horrific sin because Christ Is Better. Once Christ had come and had offered Himself as the sinless Lamb of God, no other sacrifice is necessary. Nothing else remains. You can't go back to the temple sacrifices, and you can't look forward beyond Christ for another redeemer (Romans 10:6-7). There is no other.

Jesus Christ is the fulfillment all the prophets foresaw and the angels announced. To reject Him after receiving this knowledge is to be without forgiveness because forgiveness is found in no other.

Further substantiation is found in Hebrews 10:28-29:

> *And anyone who has set aside the Law of Moses dies without mercy, on the testimony of two or three witnesses. How much severer the punishment do you think he will deserve who has trampled underfoot the Son of God, and has regarded as unclean the blood of the covenant by which he was sanctified, and has insulted the Spirit of grace?*

The writer is saying that under the Old Testament, ignoring the Law of Moses brought death as consequence. How much more is this true about Christ now that He has come?

Jesus Christ cannot be ignored. He is so much better than the Law of Moses and so much purer than the blood of bulls and goats. How much more severe the consequence if you go back?

To go back to First Covenant criteria and animal blood is to…

- ✓ trample underfoot the Son of God, Jesus Christ
- ✓ regard as unclean the blood of the New Covenant, Jesus Christ
- ✓ insult the Spirit of grace

The writer is screaming, pleading with a people on the verge of making a tragic decision. *"Don't go back! There's nothing left in the Law of works, the Levitical system, the Old Covenant Ordinances, or the animal sacrifices that can save you. Now that Christ has come, these no longer apply to you, no longer work for you and are detrimental to your salvation."*

The apostle Paul wrote in Colossians 2:13-17:

> *And when you were dead in your transgressions and the uncircumcision of your flesh, He made you alive together with Him, having forgiven us all our transgressions, having canceled out the certificate of debt consisting of decrees against us and which was hostile to us; and He has taken it out of the way, having nailed it to the cross. When He had disarmed the rulers and authorities, He made a public display of them, having triumphed over them through Him. Therefore let no one act as your judge in regard to food or drink or in respect to a festival or a new moon or a Sabbath day - things which are a mere shadow of what is to come; but the substance of what belongs to Christ.*

God's Bubble of Grace

The writer is telling these Hebrews not to insult the Spirit of grace. Now that Christ has come and has become the end of the law (Romans 10:4), going back to Law works and other blood is to insult the Spirit of Grace. It is no small matter to insult the Spirit of Grace.

Christ brought us grace—undeserved, unmerited favor. *"For the law was given through Moses, but grace and truth came through Jesus Christ"* (John 1:17 NKJV). No one can earn grace and no one deserves the gift of salvation. You don't receive grace by Law works, talents and abilities, or by educational, financial or social status. You receive it only on the merits of Jesus Christ. All we can do is receive it. Scripture informs us that if we could have earned it or deserved it, then we would boast about it:

> *But God, being rich in mercy, because of His great love with which He loved us, even when we were dead in our transgressions, made us alive together with Christ (by grace you have been saved), and raised us up with Him and seated us with Him in the heavenly places, in Christ Jesus, in order that in the ages to come He might show the surpassing riches of His grace in kindness toward us in Christ Jesus. For by grace you have been saved through faith; and that not of yourselves, it is the gift of God;* ***not as a result of works, that no one should boast***.
>
> (Ephesians 2:4-9)

Christ gives grace. God alone will receive the glory for this great gift of eternal life through Christ. We come to Him with nothing and He gives us everything. All we can do is receive His great salvation and spend our life as grateful, gracious worshippers and disciples.

See, we live in a grace bubble—a grace dispensation. The dispensations of Law and Grace have not existed simultaneously. Moses, the deliverer brought a hard dispensation of Law to the

Jews, and as man added to the Law, it became harder. The dispensation of the Law ended with Christ. *"For Christ is the end of the law for righteousness to everyone who believes"* (Romans 10:4).

We now live in the dispensation of Grace. The Age of Grace follows the age or dispensation of the Law. One follows the other, they are not merged nor do they overlap. They are two distinct dispensations in both the mind of God and the history of man.

This Age of Grace began 2000 years ago at the cross of Christ where He poured out the blood of God to redeem or buy us back and forgive our sins. Because of it, every believer in Christ enters into an amazing, undeserved arena of grace. This grace bubble begins at the cross and ends at the second coming of Christ. It begins with the advent of Christ and ends at His return.

This is an age unlike any ever seen before. Grace isn't fair in the opinion of religion, but it is wonderful and available to everyone who believes.

As diametrically opposed as Law and Grace are, their purpose is the same: To make us righteous so God can receive us into fellowship with Him. The problem with the Law is that it failed; it could not make man righteous. This is clearly pointed out in Hebrews 10:11: *"And every priest stands daily ministering and offering time after time the same sacrifices, which can never take away sins."*

Daily, the Old Testament priests offered animal sacrifices in obedience to God. The problem was, these animal sacrifices would never take away sins.

> *For the Law, since it has only a shadow of the good things to come and not the very form of things, can never by the same sacrifices year by year, which they*

> *offer continually, make perfect those who draw near. Otherwise, would they not have ceased to be offered, because the worshippers, having once been cleansed, would not longer have had consciousness of sins? But in those sacrifices there is a reminder of sins year by year. For it is impossible for the blood of bulls and goats to take away sins.*
> *(Hebrews 10:1-4)*

Instead, they served to remind the worshiper that he was a sinner and that animal sacrifices didn't work. They served to point to a supreme sacrifice that would work: Jesus Christ. Hebrews 10:12,14 declares: *"but He, having offered one sacrifice for sins for all time, sat down at the right hand of God... For by one offering He has perfected for all time those who are sanctified."*

Christ, by His eternal offering, cleansed the believer for all time. He accomplished this redemptive cleansing apart from the Law ALL BY HIMSELF. Christ is better!

Apply the Keys

Let's apply these two themes or keys to some areas in Hebrews and see how they enlighten our understanding of this marvelous Epistle and help us grasp the truths set forth in this book.

- Christ Is Better
- Don't Go Back

> *Therefore, since a promise remains of entering His rest, let us fear lest any of you seem to have come short of it. For indeed the gospel was preached to us as well as to them; but the word which they heard did not profit them, not being mixed with faith in those* (HEB 4:1-2)

[handwritten note: those that came out of Egypt, but they never entered the promised land.]

> *who heard it.*
>
> (Hebrews 4:1-2)

The recipients of this Epistle knew the story. They understood that the writer was talking about their own forefathers entering the Lord's rest after being delivered out of Egyptian bondage. They remembered how Moses confronted Pharaoh with miraculous signs and wonders in order to gain the deliverance of Israel. They knew that Moses led the people to the Red Sea and that God miraculously parted the waters so they could cross over to dry land. Furthermore, they knew how Pharaoh's army was drowned as the walls of the sea crashed over them.

The Israelites were taken out of Egyptian bondage and delivered to the doorway of their promised inheritance. They could see the abundance of this marvelous land flowing with milk and honey. Not only could they peer across the border into Canaan, but they also saw the abundant harvest brought back by the twelve Promised Land spies. The people heard Joshua and Caleb pleading with them to go in, but because of their fear and unbelief, they refused to enter in to receive their promise.

Notice how the writer used those who had already believed to entice these early Hebrew churchgoers not to refuse Christ (their promised land):

> *For we who have believed enter that rest, just as He has said, AS I SWORE IN MY WRATH, THEY SHALL NOT ENTER MY REST, although His works were finished from the foundation of the world.*
>
> (Hebrews 4:3)
>
> *Since therefore it remains for some to enter it, and those who formerly had good news preached to them failed to enter because of disobedience.*
>
> (Hebrews 4:6)

Some still needed to enter this promised rest, which is salvation in Christ.

> *Let us therefore be diligent to enter that rest, lest anyone fall through following the same example of disobedience.*
>
> (Hebrews 4:11)
>
> *And with whom was He angry for forty years? Was it not with those who sinned, whose bodies fell in the wilderness? And to whom did He swear that they should never enter His rest, but to those who were disobedient? And so we see that they were not able to enter because of their unbelief.*
>
> (Hebrews 3:17-19)

The writer pleaded with the Hebrews to enter their promised rest in Christ. He begged them to allow the Good News—to which they had mentally assented—to take root in their hearts. He urged them to mix faith with what they had heard and receive Christ in their hearts for complete and full salvation.

Chapters 3 and 4 of Hebrews appealed most urgently, as in an emergency, to those hearers not to reject Christ and His better blood, better sacrifice, and better covenant. Because of the unrelenting persecution, those who are incomplete in Christ are leaning back to the temple ritual and animal blood which will sever them from a true completion of salvation in Christ.

> *Therefore, just as the Holy Spirit says,*
>
> *"Today if you hear his voice,*
> *Do not harden your hearts as when they provoked me,*
>
> *As in the day of trial in the wilderness,*
>
> *Where your fathers tried me by testing me,*
>
> *And saw my works for forty years.*

> *"Therefore I was angry with this generation,*
>   *And said, 'they always go astray in their heart;*
>
> *And they did not know my ways';*
>
> *As I swore in my wrath,*
>
> *'They shall not enter my rest.'"*
>
> *Take care, brethren, lest there should be in any one of you <u>an evil, unbelieving heart</u>, in falling away from the living God.*
>
> (Hebrews 3:7-12)

Until the End

Two more most interesting verses in Hebrews are found in chapter 3. Again, these verses prove how vital the keys to Hebrews are if we are to understand this most important book of Scripture and the truths it contains.

> Verse 6—*But Christ was faithful as a Son over His house whose house we are, if we hold fast our confidence and the boast of our hope firm until the end.*
>
> Verse 14—*For we have become partakers of Christ, if we hold fast the beginning of our assurance firm until the end.*

The words "until the end" are important in light of the writer's urgent appeal. He speaks to the Hebrews who have heard the Good News preached to them and tells them in verse 6 "to hold fast...their confidence, and the boast of hope **until the end**." The words in verse 14 are almost identical, "if we hold fast the beginning of our assurance firm **until the end**."

The phrase "until the end" means more than a cursory reading reveals. It's not talking about the end of a person's life, but the end of the process that has begun in them. "Until the end" refers to things in the hearers life that have not yet come full circle. This speaks to the hearer who has not yet mixed with faith what they have heard and received in their hearts as salvation by Christ alone.

This phrase comes from the Greek word *telos*, which literally means "perfection" or "perfectly completed." According to the *Theological Dictionary of the New Testament*:

1. *Telos* means "achievement," "fulfillment," "execution," "success," then "power," "official power," and "office."
2. Another meaning is "completion," "perfection," "final step," "supreme stage," … "goal," … "result," "conclusion," "end"…. Adverbially the meaning is "finally," "fully," "totally"…

Telos carries with it the meaning of fulfillment, perfection, and conclusion. Knowing this, we can see that the writer expressed his supreme desire to see the readers of Hebrews come to a completion in their faith in Christ alone.

"Let Us Go on to Perfection"

Likewise, the writer states in Hebrews 6:1: *"Therefore, leaving the discussion of the elementary principles of Christ, let us go on to perfection"* (NKJV). The word "perfect" must not be interpreted "mature" in this instance. These hearers cannot go on to spiritual maturity because they have not yet been spiritually born. Something not yet born cannot mature. The writer is encouraging these undecided hearers to leave the elementary teachings **about the Christ** and to go on to perfection.

"Perfection" in Greek is *teleiotes* which stresses the actual accomplishment of the end in view. The end in view here is a person. That Person, and that destination is Jesus Christ.

The hearers are urged not to stop in their faith process, but to go on unto Christ, unto Perfection. They have mentally assented to this Good News, now they must move forward and *"mix what they have heard with faith"* (Hebrews 4:2) and accept Christ alone as their salvation. Vincent's Word studies in the New Testament offers a better translation, *"unto the consummation. It is more than mere termination. It is the point into which the whole life of faith finally gathers itself up"* (Vol. IV p. 419). That point, that consummation, is Christ.

Remember These Key Points:

1. **Grow in the Security of the Father.**

    Insecure people are very immature people. As believers grow in the security of the Father, they grow in maturity as Christians.

2. **Go for Relationship, Not Religion.**

    God wants a relationship with you. You were not created to fight through this life all alone. God's desire is to be beside you all the way, dwelling in you as your source and leading you into His fullness.

3. **Street Smart**

    Being street smart is not all it's built up to be. Usually, those who are street smart are cynical, untrusting, and insecure. God's desire is for you to be "Christ smart" as your wounds and insecurities are dealt with and and healed.

4. **Accept Fully God's Forgiveness.**

   Forgiveness is complete. God doesn't drag the bottom of His "sea of forgetfulness" to see what relics of your past He can raise before you. However, you mustn't do it either. Accept what Jesus Christ has bought for you. Don't go back!

5. **Enjoy God's Bubble of Grace.**

   You are surrounded by a bubble of grace. God's grace is so pervasive that you cannot escape it no matter where you go (Psalms 139).

6. **Apply the Keys.**

   The two major themes of Hebrews discussed in Chapter 1 are…

   - **Christ is better**
   - **Don't go back**

7. **Continue Until the End.**

   Continuing on to the end in the context of Hebrews 3 does not refer to death. Rather, it refers to continuing on to perfection, completeness, wholeness, and fullness. That perfection is a Person—Jesus Christ.

8. **Go on to Perfection.**

   Going on to perfection means to leave external religious criteria and go forward into Christ.

Chapter 3

Christ Brings a Better Faith

My head was spinning. Was this really happening? I thought we were good neighbors but my fellow citizens seemed to think otherwise. Several months before, we had submitted our request to the city to enlarge our facility. Now, we were at a public hearing where our appeal was put before the council and the residents for consideration.

I was unprepared for what I heard. "Too much traffic," said one. "The building will tower over our houses," declared another. "What kind of people will they be bringing in?" asked yet one concerned neighbor.

These were people I knew. I thought we had done them right over the years that our church had been in the neighborhood. After all, didn't we try to keep all the cars parked in our lots and not on the street? Didn't we try to help our neighbors who were in need? Didn't we reach out to them in many different ways? Didn't we...?

Even though the city approved our plans to build where we were, we had to re-think our status in the community and our Christian testimony in our city.

As I sat thinking about other alternatives we needed to consider, a thought kept creeping into my mind: "What are the boundaries of your faith?"

I didn't realize that my faith had boundaries, but I soon learned that it did. God kept calling to me: "Enlarge your coast: broaden your horizons; stretch your faith."

It was time to turn loose of my plan and embrace God's plan.

Faith of the Fathers

The message of faith in the Book of Hebrews becomes very clear as we use the proper keys to unlock its truths, and what a critical message it is: ***Christ is better.*** This important theme guided the recipients of the letter in a persecuted first century church just as it continues to guide believers in each passing generation.

The Epistle not only tells to us that Christ is better, but is also filled with many precious jewels of biblical truth. These truths serve as solid foundations that make up the undergirding of the platform of our lives. They are the truths upon which we build and then live our lives. The platform of better things.

Faith is high on the list of fundamental truths in Hebrews. So high, in fact, that when we think of faith our minds immediately go to the great chapter of faith, Hebrews 11. However, now that we have the keys to unlock the truths of Hebrews, we must use them to understand every verse and every chapter.

Let's use these keys—1) Christ is better 2) Don't go back—in our approach to Chapters 11 and 12. Chapter 11 cannot be fully understood apart from Chapter 12, and neither chapter can be understood apart from these interpretive keys.

The great Hall of Fame of the Heroes of Faith is found in Chapter 11. As you read it, you'll begin to move through an extensive list of Old Testament patriarchs and personalities who have done great things by and through faith: i.e., by faith: Abel, Enoch, Noah, Abraham, Sarah, Moses...

The writer builds a strong case in Hebrews 11 for these great men and women of faith. Nevertheless, you cannot rightly divide Chapter 11 without considering the first two verses of Chapter 12:

> *Therefore, since we have so great a cloud of witnesses surrounding us, let us also lay aside every encumbrance, and the sin which so easily entangles us, and let us run with endurance the race that is set before us, fixing our eyes on Jesus, the author and perfecter of faith, who for the joy set before Him endured the cross, despising the shame, and has sat down at the right hand of the throne of God.*

The writer opens Chapter 12 by referring to the cloud of witnesses honored in Chapter 11. He then says, *"...let us lay aside every encumbrance, and the sin which so easily entangles us, and let us run with endurance the race that is set before us."* Something had entangled these Hebrews that hindered completion of the process of salvation begun when they first heard the Word. Remember, the letter focuses primarily upon those in the first church who had mentally assented to the gospel but had not received Christ in their hearts as Savior.

Now, the writer begins to identify what they are stumbling over; the very heroes of chapter 11! He encourages them in verse 2 to "fix their eyes on Jesus." This expression "fix your eyes" comes from the Greek word, *apharao. Harao* means to "fix your eyes." Used with the prefix *ap* or *apo,* it means "to take your eyes from where they have previously been fixed and look away from what has to this point captured your attention," and to harao, "fix your eyes" on Jesus. Look away from one thing so you can see another.

The message to these Hebrews who were on the edge of going back to temple sacrifices is that they must take their eyes off of what they had fixed them on. What they had fixed their eyes on was entangling them and causing them to stumble. Furthermore, they stood in danger of committing the unpardonable sin of going back to animal sacrifices and the Law works of the Levitical system. They would be lost if they went back there, because after Christ and His great gift, there was no more sacrifice for sin.

These undecided Hebrews had fixed their eyes on the heroes of their faith. Their refusal to move their focus away and fix their eyes on Jesus was entangling them, causing them to stumble. The writer, in essence, said, *"You must take your eyes off of what you previously considered heroes of faith and fix your eyes on the Better Hero, Jesus. Christ is better."*

Christ is better than Moses; Christ is better than Abraham; Christ is better than Joseph or any other Old Testament patriarch. **Christ brings a better faith**.

Not only does Christ bring a better faith, but unlike anyone in the Hebrews 11 list, Christ is the *Archegos* or author and finisher of faith. The Greek word *archegos* is the word from which we derive "architect." Christ is the architect of faith. Christ not only used faith, but is the architect of faith. Jesus is the creator of faith, the personification of faith, and the center of all faith.

Moses, Abraham, and Joseph used faith; they used Christ's faith! Christ gave Moses faith, and Christ gave Abraham faith. Why, then should these Hebrews continue to cling to the imperfect, incomplete faith of Moses or Abraham? Reach forward and embrace a better, perfect faith, the Author and Finisher of all faith. Why go back? Why cling to something inferior? **Christ is better!**

> *But you have come...to Jesus, the mediator of a new covenant, and to the sprinkled blood which speaks better than the blood of Abel.*
>
> (Hebrews 12:22,24)

A Dangerous Call

This first century Hebrew church is not unlike the church of today. A call continually raises itself up in the church crying, "Go back!" Please understand what a dangerous call that is. Once you have received Christ and His full and free salvation, you must never go back to Law works, the Levitical system, or any external criteria of man for your salvation or spiritual maturity. Once you have begun your Holy Spirit walk of faith, you cannot and must not turn back. Don't allow anyone or anything to entice you back to Law works.

Paul understood this very well also. He knew that people would try to cling to what had been a former glory and stand in danger of losing the glory of the Son, Jesus Christ. He constantly fought against those who wooed the people back into the Law works of circumcision or other rules and regulations of the former things.

In a letter to the Galatians, Paul warned them by asking who bewitched them. To be bewitched is to be beguiled like Eve in the Garden of Eden (Genesis 3:1-7). Death was the result of that bewitching, and Paul knew that death would result from this bewitching as well.

You foolish Galatians, who has bewitched you, before whose eyes Jesus Christ was publicly portrayed as crucified? This is the only thing I want to find out from you: did you receive the Spirit by the works of the Law, or by hearing with faith? Are you so foolish? Having begun by the Spirit, are you now being perfected by the flesh? Did you suffer so many things in vain - if indeed it was in vain? Does He then, who provides you with the Spirit and works miracles among you, do it by the works of the Law, or by hearing with faith?

(Galatians 3:1-5)

The Criteria of Man

Society operates under complex written laws. Because people are basically self-centered and rebellious, laws are necessary to maintain a social structure in which people are safe and able to pursue their vocation and raise their families.

Likewise, God established laws that govern our environment and our lives. Natural laws bring order to the universe and make it possible for us to live and breathe with our feet planted firmly on the ground. However, God has chosen to give us the opportunity to live under a higher law in regard to our interaction with Him. Jesus fulfilled the written code of Law so that we can live in the Law of Love established by Him.

Unfortunately, our flesh loves the law. Carnality has a passion for external criteria and a religion of works. If we can choose the criteria and make the list, then we get to say who's in and who's out, something our religious flesh loves to do. We've seen it in the church over the years; external criteria imposed by man's religion that splits churches and creates denominations.

We're drawn to the Law like metal to a magnet because we've been married to it (we'll deal with this later) and we love to make the list! Whoever is in charge of the list is in charge of the holiness as well. Tragically, once started, the list never seems to have an end.

The list keepers get to say who's righteous, who's worthy, who's holy, and who isn't. It's religion at its worst, and it stinks in the nostrils of God. When we make the list of salvation criteria, we get to say who's saved, who's worthy of healing, and who's in line for blessing. Then, we become confused and disoriented when God doesn't follow what our criteria demands, and then blame Him when He doesn't perform.

Let's recognize this mentality of works' religion, identify it, and pull it out of our thinking. The creation of external criteria is a religious stronghold, and religion will fight to put it back in place if it's thrown out. The religious mind set and religious vocabulary abounds with "works" religion and humanistic external criteria.

> *For though we walk in the flesh, we do not war according to the flesh, for the weapons of our warfare are not of the flesh, but divinely powerful for the destruction of fortresses. We are destroying speculations and every lofty thing raised up against the knowledge of God, and we are taking every thought captive to the obedience of Christ.*
>
> (2 Corinthians 10:3-5)

The Criteria of God

Recently, I was praying for a man. I wanted him healed so badly, that in my petition to God I said, "Lord, heal this man, he's such a good man." The Lord arrested me in my tracks and rebuked me immediately. He said to me, *"I'm not going to heal him because **he's** good, I'm going to heal him because **I'm** Good!"*

I was deeply convicted. I had slipped and had pulled back into my vocabulary some external criteria. I had decided that he was a good man, and on that basis God needed to respond. However, God doesn't respond to my criteria or anyone else's. God responds to FAITH!

Jesus did not respond to religious criteria; you'll never see even one narrative in the Gospels where He did. Check out His miracles. He doesn't have His disciples go before Him and distribute applications to the crowd so He can review them before He prays, heals, or delivers. Jesus never questions a person's lifestyle, how much he or she gave, where he or she had spent the previous night and exactly what he or she had done.

Jesus Christ responds to **faith!** Consider the woman with the issue of blood. Jesus never had one question about her holiness, goodness, or heritage. He didn't say, "your prayer life has made you whole" or "your church attendance has made you whole." Jesus didn't look at her and say, "your missions giving has made you whole." No, Jesus said, "Your FAITH has made you whole." Religion responds to man-made, external criteria; God responds to faith.

> *And a woman who had had a hemorrhage for twelve years,*
>
> *and had endured much at the hands of many physicians, and had spent all that she had and was not helped at all, but rather had grown worse,*
>
> *after hearing about Jesus, came up in the crowd behind Him, and touched His cloak.*

For she thought, "If I just touch His garments, I shall get well."

And immediately the flow of her blood was dried up; and she felt in her body that she was healed of her affliction.

And immediately Jesus, perceiving in Himself that the power proceeding from Him had gone forth, turned around in the crowd and said, "Who touched My garments?"

And His disciples said to Him, "You see the multitude pressing in on You, and You say, 'Who touched Me?'"

And He looked around to see the woman who had done this.

But the woman fearing and trembling, aware of what had happened to her, came and fell down before Him, and told Him the whole truth.

And He said to her, "Daughter, your faith has made you well; go in peace, and be healed of your affliction."

faith is the magnet that draws the attention of God (Mark 5:25-34)

As a pastor, I believe that prayer, church attendance, and missions giving are very important. The existence and outreach of the church depend on these vital elements. These beliefs are so important to me they tempt me to set up my own criteria. If I did, some people would be included and others would be excluded. The church could operate and function according to me, but I'm not the last word. In fact, I'm not even the first word; I'm just a response to His Word. His Word says, *"Go your way, your faith has made you whole."* Criteria closed.

The time has come for the church to get relevant with the truth, streamline its powerful message, and turn to a dying world with a Word from God. Therefore, it's important to center your doctrine exactly on Jesus' Word. Refuse to

- espouse a list of flawed principles that have nothing to do with the Word of God.
- issue a list of Law works and a Levitical system that dictates to and weighs down believers.
- exhaust believers through striving, working, and condemning.
- suffer for something you don't believe because somebody said you should.

Your Church Can

Stop telling your church that it can't have revival until some external religious criteria is met. Stop saying:

- You haven't prayed enough.
- You haven't fasted enough.
- There's sin in the church.

[handwritten note: WRONG THEOLOGY]

Get over it! There will always be sin in the church. However, God is big enough to have revival through it and in spite of it. Stop setting your church up for failure and defeat. Start talking faith and believing God for revival. It will come if you'll believe for it.

Faith is the magnet that attracts the attention, the blessings, and the revival of God, not external religious rules. God wants to give you and your church a revival right now. So, why don't you start believing and begin expecting it? God won't bless you because you deserve it or because you are worthy. You're not worthy. Only Jesus is worthy and He alone will save your community and send you a revival.

Your assignment, your mandate isn't to get everything perfect so God will show up. <u>Your mandate is to believe.</u> God will show up in the middle of the mess. God fixes messes, and He has a revival bigger than the sin in your community and the religion in your church.

> Matthew 8:13: *"And Jesus said to the centurion, 'Go your way; let it be done to you as you have <u>believed</u>.' And the servant was healed that very hour."*

> Luke 8:49: *"But when Jesus heard this, He answered him, 'Do not be afraid any longer; <u>only believe</u>, and she shall be made well.'"*

> Mark 11:24: *"Therefore I say to you, all things for which you pray and ask, <u>believe</u> that you have received them, and they shall be granted you."*

The Boundaries of Your Faith

What are the boundaries of your faith? Have you reached the edge where your faith stops and the great unknown of Christ's faith begins? You may have reached the jumping off point, and are beckoned by the promises of God but are still unsure of what to do or when to do it. Rest assured, Jesus Christ is there and it is He who beckons and calls you.

The great cloud of witnesses in Hebrews chapter 11 is made up of people just like you and me: what set them apart was their faith in God. It's time to lay aside your criteria and your agenda, and grasp what has taken hold of you.

The apostle Paul wrestled with his boundary of faith. First, while watching Stephen being stoned, then on the road to Damascus, he saw that what he had lived for was incomplete. Paul discovered something that we all need to discover: Christ's faith is bigger than ours; Christ's love is deeper than ours, and Christ's grace is greater than ours. However, we can have His faith, we can have His love, and we can have His grace. All we have to do is receive it.

Pressing beyond your boundary of faith requires complete trust in God. It's only as you take hold of the hand of Jesus that you can truly begin to experience the depth of faith required for your journey through life. Where has God called you to go? What has He called you to do?

The faith required to do all that God has called you to do may be greater than the amount of faith you're operating in at this time. Paul said that he could do anything through Christ who strengthened him (Philippians 4:13), and reading what he wrote about the hardships he encountered in ministry bears testimony to the truth of that statement (2 Corinthians 11:16-33).

What about you? Are you willing to put your trust completely in Christ? Are you ready to step into the great unknown of your calling and let Him guide you? Christ does bring a better faith—try it. You'll like it.

By the way, the Lord had preserved nineteen beautiful acres for our church on a popular U.S. highway overlooking the Indian River. It meant moving the entire church plant and starting all over again in construction, but it was exactly what we needed to do, and where our faith needed to go. The faith required to do that was greater than the faith I was exercising at the time. But as I stepped out of my safety zone, God allowed my faith to soar to reach His desires. Jesus never fails.

Remember these key points:

1. **The Faith of the Fathers Was Dynamic.**

   Hebrews reminds us about the dynamic faith of men and women through the ages: Abel, Noah, Abraham, Joseph, Moses, Rahab, and others too numerous to mention. These heroes of faith showed that God calls people beyond where they are and then gives them the faith to accomplish what God called them to do.

2. **Going Back Is Dangerous.**

   Don't go back! This call to return to former things the Laws, the Levitical system, or the external criteria of man—is fraught with danger. Once you've begun your Holy Spirit walk of faith, you cannot and must not turn back. The recipients of the Hebrew letter were refusing to let go of their former heroes of faith to embrace the greater faith, the better faith of Jesus Christ who is the architect of faith.

3. **Man's Criteria Is a Religion of Works.**

   Carnality has a passion for external criteria and a religion of works. This leads to making lists of rules and regulations to which people must conform. Man's religion splits churches and divides denominations.

4. **God's Criteria Is Jesus' Word.**

   Center your doctrine exactly on Jesus' Word. Refuse to

   - espouse a list of flawed principles that have nothing to do with the Word of God.

- issue a list of Law works and a Levitical system that dictates to and weighs down believers.
- exhaust believers through striving, working, and condemning.
- suffer for something you don't believe because somebody said you should.

5. **Your Church Can Experience Revival.**

    Stop telling your church revival can't happen until some external religious criteria are met. Stop saying things like:
    - You haven't prayed enough.
    - You haven't fasted enough.
    - There's sin in the church.

6. **Expand the Boundaries of Your Faith.**

    Expand the boundaries of your faith. Go beyond where you are by taking hold of the hand of Jesus Christ, the author and finisher of your faith. Realize that it's in Him and Him alone that your life has meaning and purpose. Let Him show you the purpose.

Chapter 4

Is It Legal to Be Free of the Law?

I stood and greeted the lady as she walked into my office. Rita, my secretary, introduced her to me as I shook her hand and welcomed her. As I took my seat behind my desk, I sensed the tension as she made small talk trying to get comfortable. I did my best to help with the small talk while Rita took a seat over to the side, as was her custom when a woman was in my office.

As we talked, I learned that she had been attending the church for a few weeks. She started out somewhat complimentary, but quickly transitioned to the reason why she was there. Her kind but thin veneer began to melt away the closer she came to the heart of the reason why this visit was necessary.

She told me that the church and its message were OK...as far as it went. The problem, it seemed, was that my messages just didn't go far enough—they were too full of grace. She said that I needed to move on to the real stuff of the Bible so that our members could wake up, straighten out, and start living right.

The fact that she couldn't get her point across was more than her emotions could bear. She had come as a prophet to "straighten me out" and adjust this message of grace I was preaching. When she saw that I wasn't receiving her message, she started turning to the Scriptures to prove her point. Realizing that I wouldn't allow her to use the Bible to whip me and that I wasn't hearing her message, she broke into a sobbing, mournful, wailing prayer over me which I immediately interrupted by standing and inviting her out of my office. Then as she left, I was reminded again that we're all born in the Law, but we don't have to stay there.

Married to the Law

Every baby that comes into this world is born married to the Law. Yes, I know how cute and cuddly babies are, but watch them grow and you'll see that as they mature, their flesh, or carnal nature rush headlong toward Law works. The hard fact of life we must face is this: our carnal flesh nature is married to the Law from birth. Paul said:

Or do you not know, brethren (for I am speaking to those who know the law), that the law has jurisdiction over a person as long as he lives?

For the married woman is bound by law to her husband while he is living; but if her husband dies, she is released from the law concerning the husband.

So then if, while her husband is living, she is joined to another man, she shall be called an adulteress; but if her husband dies, she is free from the law, so that she is not an adulteress, though she is joined to another man.

Therefore, my brethren, you were also made to die to the Law through the body of Christ, that you might be joined to another, to Him who was raised from the dead, that we might bear fruit for God.

But now we have been released from the Law, having died to that by which we were bound, so that we serve in newness of the Spirit and not in the oldness of the letter.

(Romans 7:1-4,6)

Paul used marriage as an example of our flesh relationship with the Law. Being married to the Law from birth means we can only be freed from our Law-marriage by death—we must die.

Paul said we did die when we received Christ as our personal Savior. We died because that act identified us with Jesus in His death on the cross. Paul says that this death set us free and separated us from our former marriage.

We identify with Christ's resurrection through our new birth in Him. Thus we come alive and are now married to Him. We live as blood washed, Spirit-born believers and are *"joined to another, to Him who was raised from the dead."*

This is wonderful. It causes me to desire to worship the Lord right now for this marvelous work of redemptive deliverance bought through His death and resurrection. Not only did Jesus bring deliverance from the bondage of sin and the domain of darkness, He simultaneously brought deliverance from the Law as well.

No longer are you in bondage to legalistic commandments or the condemnation of the Levitical system's dead ceremonialism. You are set free to live your life in the freedom of Jesus' life, love, and liberty.

And when you were dead in your transgressions and

> *the uncircumcision of your flesh, He made you alive together with Him, having forgiven us all of our transgressions,*
>
> *having canceled out the certificate of debt consisting of decrees against us and which was hostile to us; and He has taken it out of the way, having nailed it to the cross.*
>
> *When He had disarmed the rulers and authorities, He made a public display of them, having triumphed over them through Him.*
>
> *Therefore, let no one act as your judge in regard to food or drink or in respect to a festival or a new moon or a Sabbath day—*
>
> *things which are a mere shadow of what is to come...."*
>
> (Colossians 2:13-17)

Jesus Christ *"canceled out the certificate of debt"* against you. He *"has taken it out of the way, having nailed it to the cross"* so don't go back. Don't go back to an external legalistic system of religious criteria that will judge you *"in regard to food or drink or in respect to a festival or a new moon, or a Sabbath day."* Don't go back to a place where people can set themselves up as judge over you in these things. The Bible speaks so clearly on this issue, there is no reason to be confused.

The Law Lives

Be sure of this: though you died to the Law and were resurrected married to Christ, *the Law isn't dead*. The spirit of legalism and external Law works continue very much alive today. Even though you are now married to Christ, the Law will come and flirt with you to woo you back.

Don't go back! Don't allow anyone to turn your head from the grace that Jesus Christ offers through Himself. No matter what anyone says to you about your relationship with Christ, you must remember that Jesus is your Savior and He is enough all by Himself. You don't need the add-ons or external criteria touted by present day Judaizers. They are always around and always ready to load you down.

Yes, the Law lives. This legalism comes in many forms and seeks to bind you hand and foot to a form of "holiness" that is hollow and fruitless. The criterion of man always falls far short of the criteria of God. Where Christ offers grace, legalism promises judgment. Where Christ offers love, Judaizers promise hate. Where Christ offers unity, Law works promise separation.

When Jesus said He came to fulfill the Law (Matthew 5:17), He bore the brunt of the heavy hand of a legalistic religious system. As this heavy hand of judgment pummeled Him with blow after blow, the work of grace was overcoming the works of the Law.

When Jesus cried out from the cross "It is finished," grace triumphed and legalism was vanquished. Our promise is very clear: *"For God did not send His Son into the world to condemn the world, but that the world through Him might be saved"* (John 3:17 NKJV).

The Judaizers

Notice Peter's first encounter with the Judaizers:

Now the apostles and the brethren who were

> *throughout Judea heard that the Gentiles also had received the word of God.*
>
> *And when Peter came up to Jerusalem, those who were circumcised took issue with him, saying, "You went to uncircumcised men and ate with them."*

(Acts 11:1-3)

These verses introduce the Judaizers of the New Testament. Acts 15 gives clear insight into them and into their teachings. *"And some men came down from Judea and began teaching the brethren, 'Unless you are circumcised according to the custom of Moses, you cannot be saved'"* (Acts 15:1).

The name "Judaizers" means they "came down from Judea," or more specifically from Jerusalem where Peter first encountered them (Acts 11). Acts 15:2 shows that they were causing "great dissension" which is what they continue to do today. In fact, the Judaizers caused so much dissension concerning Paul's revelation of grace and subsequent preaching that both he and Barnabas traveled to Jerusalem to discuss the matter.

The following verse provides two interesting insights into these men: *"But certain ones of the sect of the Pharisees who had believed, stood up, saying, 'It is necessary to circumcise them, and to direct them to observe the Law of Moses'"* (Acts 15:5).

Insight #1: They are identified as believers.

These men were Pharisees who seemed to have come to belief in Christ. However, when Paul clarified this account of the Jerusalem conference of Acts 15, he called them false brethren. Paul declared:

> *But it was because of the false brethren who had sneaked in to spy out our liberty which we have in Christ Jesus, in order to bring us into bondage. But*

> *we did not yield in subjection to them for even an hour, so that the truth of the gospel might remain with you.*
>
> (Galatians 2:4-5)

Paul identified these Judaizers correctly. They were then, as they are now, busy about stealing away your freedom in Christ.

Remember: grace comes to bring you freedom *in* Christ, not *from* Christ. The goal of grace is the same as the goal of the Old Testament Law—righteousness. The difference is the Old Testament Law failed to produce righteousness in people. Why? Because it's more than just conforming to a written set of rules. Therefore, what the Law failed to do, Christ and His blood succeeded in doing. Grace succeeds.

It is ridiculous to consider that the message of grace provides a license for loose living or the absence of discipline and godly principles. Grace is not the presence of hedonism, but the absence of legalism. The arena of grace does not celebrate flesh; grace celebrates Christ's life and love. A person's love for Christ constrains him from a life of carnal rebellion and sin.

Grace comes to fill you with God's love and righteousness. Through grace, you now have right standing with God. He now lives in your heart to empower your life in His fullness, holiness, and godly obedience. Where the Law fails, God's grace succeeds. Righteousness can only come through faith in Jesus Christ. God stipulates no other avenue to His righteousness.

> *For the promise to Abraham or to his descendants that he would be heir of the world was not through the Law, but through the righteousness of faith.*
>
> *For if those who are of the Law are heirs, faith is made void and the promise is nullified;*
>
> *for the Law brings about wrath, but where there is no*

law, neither is there violation.
(Romans 4:13-15)

The promise that we are to be heirs of the world comes not through Law works, but through faith in Christ alone. The Law not only fails to produce righteousness, but the Law brings about wrath.

Insight #2: Their list of do's and don'ts is never-ending.

The nature of the spirit of the Judaizers is revealed in what they demand the people do. Acts 15:1 reveals their command that circumcision be added to Christ for salvation: *"unless you are circumcised according to the custom of Moses, you cannot be saved."* By the time they get to Jerusalem in verse 5, they demand them to not only be circumcised, but also, *"to observe the Law of Moses."* This reveals the spirit that drives this Judaizing religion—its list is never long enough and once it gets started, there is no end.

The Jerusalem Conference

Acts 15

The Jerusalem Conference was a vital and pivotal meeting for this young, fledgling church. It was at a crisis crossroads and had the apostles not made right decisions, the New Testament Church would have become no more than an arm of the Levitical Law system. If this would have happened, it would have ultimately led to a total failure in respect to what Christ came to establish and purchase with His blood on Calvary (Acts 20:28).

These were critical times. Heavy responsibility was being forced on the inexperienced leaders of this young church. The wrong decision would have weighed down the New Testament church with Law works, Levitical ceremonies, and dead tradition. With wrong decisions the first church would have suffocated and ceased to exist, and Christ's coming would have been of no effect (Galatians 5:4 KJV). However, proper decisions would separate once and for all what was becoming the international New Testament church from the Judaistic ceremonialism of Old Testament death and condemnation (Romans 7:10; 2 Corinthians 3:7).

The tension builds in Acts 15 as we approach the decision of the Jerusalem Conference. We read on holding our breath and whispering prayers that the leaders of this new movement will make righteous, eternally correct decisions.

The Holy Spirit led the council, and with great wisdom they profoundly and unequivocally embraced the message of grace and freedom. This was the same revelation message being preached by Paul throughout the region. Peter's words lay a strong foundation for this message of grace against the Law:

> *And God, who knows the heart, bore witness to them, giving them the Holy Spirit, just as He also did to us;*
>
> *and He made no distinction between us and them, cleansing their hearts by faith.*
>
> *Now therefore why do you put God to the test by placing upon the neck of the disciples a yoke which neither our fathers nor we have been able to bear?*
>
> (Acts 15:8-10)

Peter's words concerning the former Old Covenant Levitical Law system recap what every one of the men there knew: *"why do you put God to the test by placing upon the neck of the disciples a yoke that neither our fathers nor we have been able to bear?"* He said that the Old Covenant, the Law works, didn't do what they were supposed to do. Instead, the yoke choked their fathers. Why pass this choking yoke of bondage on and taint this new and wonderful thing God has done?

This decision dealt a major blow to the old Levitical system and it having any power over the New Testament church. Peter's words rang the bell of liberty that set believers free from the yoke of Law bondage, and this liberty bell of the church continues to ring down through the centuries. These clear statements are unmistakable. The New Testament Church is not a carryover of Old Testament Judaism, but a completely new beginning with a completely new and living message.

James expressed the final word for the Jerusalem conference: *"Therefore, it is my judgment that we do not trouble those who are turning to God from among the Gentiles"* (Acts 15:19). James declared that these new believers adhere to righteous requirements and abstain from:

- idolatry
- fornication
- blood (murder)

James further endorses Paul and the New Testament message as he distances the Jerusalem church and its leadership from these Judaizers: *"Since we have heard that some of our number to whom **we gave no instruction** have disturbed you with their words, unsettling your souls"* (Acts 15:24). He makes it clear that, while these men claimed credentials from the Jerusalem church to spread their Judaizing heresy wherever Paul was preaching, the church had given "no instruction" or permission for them to unsettle souls with their message.

This was an incredible eternal victory for Christ and His church. We must never allow this brilliant beacon of victory to be dimmed by calls to go back to the Law and its external criteria.

So, when they were sent away, they went down to Antioch; and having gathered the congregation together, they delivered the letter.

And when they had read it, they rejoiced because of its encouragement.

(Acts 15:30-31)

Paul's Thorn

The Jerusalem Conference of Acts 15 settled the issue for the leadership and established the true message of the New Testament church. However, it by no means silenced the heretical voices of the Judaizers. Nor did it quench their unrelenting insistence to add to the Gospel the heavy baggage and troublesome burdens of first covenant demands.

The Epistles of Paul deal primarily with troubling issues in the young first century churches stirred up by these tormenting Judaizers. They became Paul's thorn in the flesh and waged continual, relentless assault on his message of grace, liberty and salvation through Christ alone.

For I am jealous for you and with a godly jealousy; for I betrothed you to one husband, that to Christ I might present you as a pure virgin.

But I am afraid, lest as the serpent deceived Eve by his craftiness, your minds should be led astray from the simplicity and purity of devotion to Christ.

For such men are false apostles, deceitful workers, disguising themselves as apostles of Christ.

And no wonder, for even Satan disguises himself as an angel of light.

> *Therefore it is not surprising if his servants also disguise themselves as servants of righteousness; whose end shall be according to their deeds.*
>
> (2 Corinthians 11:2-3,13-15)

The words of verse 2 concerning the believer's betrothal to Christ speak of the same relationship as Romans 7:1-4. These believers have died to the Law and have now been married to Christ.

Paul's warning to them is not to allow the legalists to deceive them (v. 3) and to turn them away from the simplicity that is in Christ. Paul has no patience with these false apostles who moved among the church to unsettle these young believers. He calls the first covenant bondage they preach the ministry of death in letters engraved on stones.

> *But if the ministry of death, in letters engraved on stones, came with glory, so that the sons of Israel could not look intently at the face of Moses because of the glory of his face, fading as it was,*
>
> *how shall the ministry of the spirit fail to be even more with glory?*
>
> *For if the ministry of condemnation has glory, much more does the ministry of righteousness abound in glory.*
>
> *For indeed what had glory, in this case has no glory on account of the glory that surpasses it.*
>
> (2 Corinthians 3:7-10)

Paul worked hard and suffered much to lead these precious ones out of bondage into the truth of Christ and His glorious freedom. No words can describe the pain he suffered as he realized the work of dissension being carried out among them.

Let's examine some of what Paul wrote to these believers and seek to capture the depth of passion he had for them and the message he imparted to them:

> *I am amazed that you are so quickly deserting Him who called you by the grace of Christ, for a different gospel;*
>
> *which is really not another; only there are some who are disturbing you, and want to distort the gospel of Christ.*
>
> *But even though we, or an angel from heaven, should preach to you a gospel contrary to that which we have preached to you, let him be accursed.*
>
> *As we have said before, so I say again now, if any man is preaching to you a gospel contrary to that which you received, let him be accursed.*
>
> (Galatians 1:6-9)
>
> *Nevertheless knowing that a man is not justified by the works of the Law, but through faith in Christ Jesus, even we have believed in Christ Jesus, that we may be justified by faith in Christ, and not by the works of the Law; since by the works of the Law shall no flesh be justified.*
>
> *I do not nullify the grace of God; for if righteousness comes through the Law, then Christ died needlessly.*
>
> (Galatians 2:16,21)
>
> *You foolish Galatians, who has bewitched you, before whose eyes Jesus Christ was publicly portrayed as crucified?*
>
> *This is the only thing I want to find out from you: did you receive the Spirit by the works of the Law, or by*

hearing with faith?

Are you so foolish? Having begun by the Spirit, are you now being perfected by the flesh?

Did you suffer so many things in vain—if indeed it was in vain?

Does He then, who provides you with the Spirit and works miracles among you, do it by the works of the Law, or by hearing with faith?

(Galatians 3:1-5)

For as many as are of the works of the Law are under a curse; for it is written, 'cursed is everyone who does not abide by all things written in the book of the law, to perform them.'

Now that no one is justified by the Law before God is evident; for, 'the righteous man shall live by faith.

However, the Law is not of faith; on the contrary, 'he who practices them shall live by them.'

Christ redeemed us from the curse of the Law, having become a curse for us—for it is written, 'cursed is everyone who hangs on a tree'—

in order that in Christ Jesus the blessing of Abraham might come to the Gentiles, so that we might receive the promise of the Spirit through faith...

Therefore the Law has become our tutor to lead us to Christ, that we may be justified by faith.

But now that faith has come, we are no longer under a tutor.

For you are all sons of God through faith in Christ Jesus.

For all of you who were baptized into Christ have clothed yourselves with Christ.

There is neither Jew nor Greek, there is neither slave nor free man, there is neither male nor female; for you are all one in Christ Jesus.

(Galatians 3:10-14, 24-28)

C.I. Schofield wrote:

The test of the gospel is grace. If the message excludes grace, or mingles law with grace as the means, either of justification or sanctification, it is "another" gospel and the preacher of it is under the anathema of God.

Paul's words in Galatians 5 remind us again of the profound warning to be free from the legalism of the Judaizers.

It was for freedom that Christ set us free; therefore keep standing firm and do not be subject again to a yoke of slavery.

Behold I, Paul, say to you that if you receive circumcision, Christ will be of no benefit to you.

And I testify again to every man who receives circumcision, that he is under obligation to keep the whole Law.

You have been severed from Christ, you who are seeking to be justified by law; you have fallen from grace.

For we through the Spirit, by faith, are waiting for the hope of righteousness.

For in Christ Jesus neither circumcision nor uncircumcision means anything, but faith working through love.

You were running well; who hindered you from obeying the truth?

This persuasion did not come from Him who calls you.

A little leaven leavens the whole lump of dough.

I have confidence in you in the Lord, that you will adopt no other view; but the one who is disturbing you shall bear his judgment, whoever he is.

(Galatians 5:1-10)

Messengers of Satan

Hostile forces surrounded Paul on every side. Tragically, many of these enemies were in the church. It's bad enough to fight the enemy you know to be there, but when you're attacked from within it seems to hurt especially bad.

And because of the surpassing greatness of the revelations, for this reason, to keep me from exalting myself, there was given to me a thorn in the flesh, a messenger of Satan to buffet me—to keep me from exalting myself!

Concerning this I entreated from the Lord three times that it might depart from me.

And He has said to me, "My grace is sufficient for you, for power is perfected in weakness."

Most gladly, therefore, I will rather boast about my weaknesses, that the power of Christ may dwell in me.

(2 Corinthians 12:7-9)

That these verses are found in 2 Corinthians is interesting. Their location is a clue in identifying Paul's thorn in the flesh. Paul wrote 2 Corinthians after meeting Titus in Macedonia: *"I had no rest for my spirit, not finding Titus my brother; but taking my leave of them, I went on to Macedonia"* (2 Corinthians 2:13). *"For even when we came into Macedonia our flesh had no rest, but we were afflicted on every side: conflicts without, fears within"* (2 Corinthians 7:5-6). Paul's problem was that he couldn't return to Corinth because of the great Judaizing problem in the church. He wasn't welcome and may have even been in danger by arriving in Corinth prematurely.

The comfort that Titus brought to Paul was the news that Titus had cleared the way for Paul's return. Once there, he could embrace the church that he had founded and they would embrace him. Titus did a thorough job of ridding the Corinthian church of the divisive Judaizers who had brought so much dissension to the body.

Paul's heart was comforted and overjoyed by the news from Titus that he could return to Corinth:

> *And not only by his coming, but also by the comfort with which he was comforted in you, as he reported to us your longing, your mourning, your zeal for me; so that I rejoiced even more...*
>
> *For behold what earnestness this very thing, this godly sorrow, has produced in you: what vindication of yourselves, what indignation, what fear, what longing, what zeal, what avenging of wrong! In everything you demonstrated yourselves to be innocent in the matter...*
>
> *For this reason we have been comforted.*
>
> (2 Corinthians 7:7,11,13)

Paul's comments are filled with gratitude that the destructive presence of the Judaizers has been eradicated from the church. Furthermore, he's happy that these believers have vindicated themselves and have even demonstrated their innocence in this entire matter.

Armed with this knowledge, it's easier to understand why in this same letter we have Paul's comments concerning his thorn in the flesh (2 Corinthians 12:7). This insight, along with the evident suffering Paul has endured from these Judaizers reveal who, not what, Paul's thorn in the flesh was. These Judaizers were messengers sent from Satan to buffet him.

In continuing to identify Paul's thorn in the flesh, it is important that he personifies his tormentors. In *Word Studies*…Vincent says the: "Messenger…is the word commonly rendered angel in the New Testament, though sometimes used of human messengers, as Luke 7:24,27; 9:52, James 2:25."

Concerning the word *"buffet,"* Robertson says: "The messenger of Satan kept slapping Paul in the face…"

This personification is not wasted on this illustration. Paul's thorn was not sickness or disease, but human messengers who sought to nullify his revelation of Grace.

Jesus Responds to Paul

Paul's prayer regarding these tormentors is recorded in verse 8 where he asked the Lord three times to have this assault removed (vs. 7). Paul doesn't clearly identify the subject of his prayer although the Lord's answer makes the subject quite clear: "And He has said to me, 'My grace is sufficient for you" (2 Corinthians 12:9). Don't miss the subject matter of the Lord's answer—GRACE.

You can identify the subject of the question by the subject of the answer. For instance, if someone asked your friend a question that you didn't hear but you heard the answer, you could probably figure out the question. If your friend answered, "I'm sorry, we're out of milk," you would be correct in assuming the question was about milk. If the subject of the answer was money, you could be assured the question was about money. The same is true in Paul's request to the Lord.

The Lord's answer identifies Paul's request—*"my grace is sufficient...."* If Paul would have asked the Lord about healing, the Lord would have responded with healing, not grace. If Paul had entreated the Lord about finances, the Lord would have responded about finances, not grace.

Therefore, it's obvious that Paul talked to the Lord about grace praying something like this: "Please remove these people from me who frustrate the message and revelation of grace You gave me." The Lord didn't promise to remove them, but He promised that the message of grace that He had revealed to Paul was sufficient for him. Grace was sufficient to withstand every attack of the Judaizers and every onslaught of religion.

God's grace is sufficient. It isn't weak, it isn't emaciated, nor does it lack ability to overcome. Grace isn't fragile. It's sufficient. Grace will make it through attack.

When the smoke clears and the dust settles, grace will be standing strong. The Lord Jesus cries out, "My grace is sufficient." It will fully accomplish and complete what God has designed it to do.

Judaizers were, and still are today, a thorn in the side and a slap in the face to this message of grace. However, nothing will stop what God has begun. His Word will not return to Him void, but will succeed in the matter to which He sent it.

His Grace Is Sufficient for You Too

Are you surrounded by Judaizers? Do you feel the onslaught of those who would seek to thwart the truth of God and the message of grace within you? Are you pounded by the breakers of an angry sea of protesters who demand a return to the ways of the Law?

Shake it off! Jesus bore all that they could throw at Him or anyone else and defeated them at their own game. The spirit of the Judaizer is the same that was in the serpent in the Garden of Eden. They live in the Tree of Knowledge of Good and Evil, the tree of judgment, and seek to have you spend your life judging yourself, others, and even God.

Judgment is the way of death, not life. Judgment brings distance, discord, despair, and destruction. Judgment kills. Therefore, we don't depend on our own understanding but instead depend on the arms of Jesus. For His *"strength is made perfect in [our] weakness"* (2 Corinthians 12:9 NKJV).

Take hold of this gift of grace today just as you took hold of the gift of salvation. You need grace everyday just like you need air, water, and food. Grace is such a basic thing that it's like the air that you breathe, filling you with life-giving strength to go another mile.

Take it. Apprehend it. Make it yours. It's God's gift to you.

Remember these points:

1. **Don't Be Married to the Law.**

    Paul used marriage as an example of our flesh relationship with the Law. Being married to the Law from birth means we can only be freed from our Law marriage by death—we must die. We die when we receive Christ as our personal Savior.

2. **The Law Lives.**

    You died to the Law and were resurrected to Christ, but *the Law isn't dead*. The spirit of legalism and external Law works continue very much alive today.

3. **The Judaizers Will Demand That You Do.**

    Judaizers are identified as believers; they were Pharisees who came to belief in Christ. The nature of the spirit of the Judaizers is revealed in what they demand the people do, adhere to the Old Testament Law.

4. **The Jerusalem Conference Moved Us Toward Grace.**

    The Jerusalem Conference was a vital and pivotal meeting for the young, fledgling church. It was at a crossroads and had the apostles not made the right decisions, the New Testament church would have become no more than an arm of the Levitical Law system.

5. **Paul's Thorn—Legalistic People**

    The Epistles of Paul deal primarily with troubling issues that were stirred up by tormenting Judaizers. They became Paul's thorn in the flesh and waged continual, relentless assault on his message of grace, liberty and salvation through Christ alone.

6. **Messengers of Satan Will Bring Suffering**

    Paul endured great suffering at the hand of Judaizers who were Paul's thorn in the flesh. They were the messengers sent from Satan to buffet him and to keep him humble.

7. **Jesus Responds to Paul**

   Jesus understood the prayer of Paul—it was about grace. Jesus' answer was about grace as well. God's grace is sufficient. It isn't weak, it isn't emaciated, nor does it lack ability to overcome. Grace isn't fragile. It's sufficient. Grace will make it through attack.

8. **His Grace Is Sufficient for You Too.**

   Take hold of this gift of grace today just as you took hold of the gift of salvation. You need grace everyday just like you need air, water, and food. Grace is such a basic thing that it's like the air that you breathe, filling you with life-giving strength to go another mile.

Chapter 5

Salvation, God's Gift to You

"Do you have it?" the man asked. "It's three o'clock and I'm here to collect."

"I'm short $10,000." Steve said. Trying to look calm; he asked for a little more time though he knew that it wouldn't be enough. "Will you come back tomorrow?"

The debt was so great and Steve's inability to pay was so obvious that he knew he was only stalling the inevitable. Frantically, he looked for a way out but only found closed doors. He was trapped.

"No!" came the reply. "I've already extended your time twice. I'm not going to do it again."

"Can't we negotiate this again? I'm good for the money, I just need more time." Steve pleaded.

"No! Your time is up. If you don't have all the money, you lose. Now, give me what you have and give me the deed to your house. You'll have three days to clear out."

Desperate, Steve tried to bargain with the man in front of him. "But...My family. Where will we go? I've got small children. We can't be put out on the

> *street. I don't know what to do! Help me! Please help me!"*

Like Steve, we too are faced with a dilemma. Our debt of sin is too great to pay and we are unable to prevent the inevitable. No matter how long we put it off, the debt continues to grow and we become less and less able to pay.

Religion tells us to do more, comply more, walk this way, talk that way, sit here, go there, and the list goes on and on. Tragically, the more we work, the further behind we get. We cannot escape the weight of our sin no matter how long we put it off.

It's very easy to lose sight of the people when all you see is the "bottom line." Are you more concerned with collecting the debt or seeing those immersed in it set free?

Imagine that it's you in the story and not Steve. Imagine how helpless you would feel in a similar situation. In fact, you may have been in a similar situation and know firsthand the frustration, anger, fear, and helplessness that he feels.

Now imagine that someone you don't even know brings you the funds necessary to clear the debt—all the debt, not just the $10,000. Imagine further that this benefactor requires nothing on your part, no outstanding note to pay in the future, no interest or usury, no collateral to put up, nothing. When you ask Him why, He simply says: "Because I love you."

Reject Religion—Embrace the People

When you receive Jesus Christ, He puts His love in your heart for all people. God loves the world, and not only in a general sense—He loves each and every person individually.

Furthermore, God leads you to love and receive every person in **His** love and acceptance. However, God's love and acceptance of people both individually and corporately does not include embracing their religion.

Judaism is not Christianity; it is a religion as are other world religions. Judaism was the matrix which produced Christianity, just as Romanism served as a matrix which produced Reformation. Nevertheless, what was birthed out of these environments was something totally distinct and different. Follow the life of Paul and you will realize that Judaism despised, rejected and persecuted the Christianity he preached just as Romanism despised, rejected and persecuted Martin Luther's Reformation.

I have a great love for the Jewish people and the Holy Land. I look forward to the day when God turns again toward them as a nation, and when they will recognize and receive Jesus as Messiah. Meanwhile, every individual Jew who receives Christ, just as every Gentile who receives Christ, is a new creation, washed by the blood and in-filled with the Holy Spirit. However, to love and embrace the Jewish people and their Holy Land is a world apart from embracing their Law and Levitical System of external legalism and commandments.

Paul's Heart's Desire

Paul clearly separated his love for his fellow Jews from love of their religion. He made this very clear in his letter to the church at Rome:

> *Brethren, my heart's desire and my prayer to God for them is their salvation. For I bear them witness that they have zeal for God, but not in accordance with*

> *knowledge. For not knowing about God's righteousness, and seeking to establish their own, they did not subject themselves to the righteousness of God. For Christ is the end of the law for righteousness to everyone who believes.*
>
> (Romans 10:1-4)

This Jew of all Jews had a heavy heart concerning his brethren. He not only prayed for their salvation but went to them first as well. Time after time in city after city, Paul preached Jesus Christ to them and this revelation of grace. Although individual Jews received his message and his Christ, as a nation his brethren rejected him and severely persecuted him. However, their treatment of him never stopped his continual prayer regarding their salvation.

Did Paul's separation from their legalism and Law works and their subsequent persecution of him mean he was anti-Semitic? Of course not! Paul was a Jew. He loved the Jews and prayed for their salvation. However, he no longer embraced their temple, their worship, their ceremonialism, their dogma, their Law, or their legalism. He loved them, but his love for them did not blind him to their gross error and dead religion.

Paul wrote in Romans 10:2 that his brethren *"have a zeal for God, but not in accordance with knowledge."* I'm sure as he wrote this he recalled his own zeal as he persecuted Christians in the first century Church, all the while thinking he was pleasing God and doing God's work. Paul was stricken blind on the road to Damascus at the height of his religious, Pharisaical zeal to persecute Christians. At this place, Jesus Christ revealed to him the awful error of his way. Paul repented, received his sight, and became obedient to Christ.

> *Now Saul, still breathing threats and murder against the disciples of the Lord, went to the high priest,*

and asked for letters from him to the synagogues at Damascus, so that if he found any belonging to the Way, both men and women, he might bring them bound to Jerusalem.

And it came about that as he journeyed, he was approaching Damascus, and suddenly a light from heaven flashed around him;

and he fell to the ground, and heard a voice saying to him, "Saul, Saul, why are you persecuting Me?"

And he said, "Who art Thou, Lord?" And He said, "I am Jesus whom you are persecuting,

but rise, and enter the city, and it shall be told you what you must do."

(Acts 9:1-6)

Three Shortcomings of the Jewish Religion

Paul identified three areas in Romans 10:3 where the Jews fell short in their religion.

Shortcoming #1: They didn't know about Jesus' righteousness.

This not knowing wasn't because of not hearing. Paul repeatedly told them about the new righteousness revealed to him through faith in Jesus Christ *alone*. It's not that they hadn't heard; they had turned a deaf, unbelieving ear.

Shortcoming #2: They sought to establish their own righteousness.

Absolutely. Irrefutably. Any generation who will not accept Jesus Christ as their righteousness will inevitably establish their own external standards and laws.

During 1979-1980, some citizens of the United States were held hostage in Iran. I remember watching the news as these Moslem extremists marched in cadence, beating themselves on the back with whips. Because they have not accepted Christ and His forgiveness, this activity of their religion was necessary to beat the evil out of them.

This is tragic. Our great Savior Jesus Christ took the beating for us as our substitute. When we accept what He did, we will not attempt to do it for ourselves. Christ alone is our righteousness and He alone has paid our debt. We cannot and must not spend our lives attempting ourselves to pay it. Any religion, any church, anyone who does not understand this will be demanding a payment they cannot pay, but one that has already been paid.

Shortcoming #3: They did not subject themselves to the righteousness of God.

Anyone or any group who does not accept the payment of Christ's life poured out at Calvary for their complete and ultimate pardon now and forevermore are rebels of the worst kind. These religious rebels spend their lives striving and earning, demanding and judging because they don't realize they've been imputed righteousness by the Righteous One Himself. To refuse Christ's righteousness means to act out Hebrews 10:29 and

- trample underfoot the son of God
- regard as unclean the blood of the covenant
- insult the Spirit of Grace

Paul wasted no words regarding his faith in Christ and its relationship to the Law: *"For Christ is the end of the law for righteousness to everyone who believes"* (Romans 10:4). Christ spells the **end of the Law** for righteousness. For the New Testament believer, there is no righteousness in the Law; our righteousness is in Christ. When it comes to righteousness, Christ is better—don't go back.

The Debt Collector

Refusing to accept the great gift of salvation purchased by Jesus Christ at Calvary as sufficient causes you to go through life amassing debt and then striving to pay that debt when it has already been paid. Likewise, accepting the gift without realizing the full impact of what it has bought you and brought you leads to the same result. Jesus taught about debt and forgiveness in the parable of the unforgiving servant:

> *For this reason the kingdom of heaven may be compared to a certain king who wished to settle accounts with his slaves.*
>
> *And when he had begun to settle them, there was brought to him one who owed him ten thousand talents.*
>
> *But since he did not have the means to repay, his lord commanded him to be sold, along with his wife and*

children and all that he had, and repayment to be made.

The slave therefore falling down, prostrated himself before him, saying, "Have patience with me, and I will repay you everything."

And the lord of that slave felt compassion and released him and forgave him the debt.

But that slave went out and found one of his fellow slaves who owed him a hundred denarii; and he seized him and began to choke him, saying, "Pay back what you owe."

So his fellow slave fell down and began to entreat him, saying, "Have patience with me and I will repay you."

He was unwilling however, but went and threw him in prison until he should pay back what was owed.

So when his fellow slaves saw what had happened, they were deeply grieved and came and reported to their lord all that had happened.

Then summoning him, his lord said to him, "You wicked slave, I forgave you all that debt because you entreated me.

'Should you not also have had mercy on your fellow slave, even as I had mercy on you?"

And his lord, moved with anger, handed him over to the torturers until he should repay all that was owed him.

(Matthew 18:23-34)

We can quickly recognize the players in this parable. Jesus said, *"a certain King... wished to settle accounts with his slaves."* He told this story about Himself and used it to reveal who He was to all those gathered around listening.

This is an awesome revelation of King Jesus who wished *"to settle accounts with His slaves."* King Jesus stood up from the Throne of God, wrapped Himself in a robe of flesh, and took an earth walk for 33$^1/_2$ years. Jesus moved into our world, born of a virgin, and announced by angels. He walked among us, was crucified on a gory, felon's cross between two thieves and then was buried in a borrowed tomb. He rose the third day alive forevermore so He could once and for all settle the debt with His slaves!

Notice how Jesus used powerful word pictures in this parable to move the emotions of those who heard it. Let's examine it in more detail:

> **Verse 24:** *"And when he began to settle them, there was brought to him one who owed him ten thousands talents."*

Ten thousand talents is an unimaginable amount of money. One talent of silver was worth more that fifteen years of a laborer's wages! Ten thousand talents is equal to approximately $10,000,000 in silver content and is worth much more in buying power today. This situation is hilarious—it's designed to be funny. This is a ludicrous amount of money. Yes, it's a lot of money today, but it was unheard of 2000 years ago. There wasn't that much money in the world of the hearers of the parable. Listen as they start laughing. No one could ever pay that amount in a thousand lifetimes.

> **Verse 25:** *"But since he did not have the means to repay, his lord commanded him to be sold, along with*

his wife and children and all that he had, and repayment to be made."

Watch Jesus. The atmosphere has changed. Suddenly, it's become very serious and it isn't a joke any longer. It's not funny and it's unfair. No one has this amount of money, and now he, his wife and his children, will be put in slavery. If you can't pay it while you're free to work, how can you ever earn it bound in slavery? See how Jesus has this crowd right where He wants them. He goes on.

Verse 26: *"The slave therefore falling down, prostrated himself before him saying, 'Have patience with me, and I will repay you everything.'"*

Laughter time again. This poor soul actually thinks he can work off this unbelievable mountain of debt. Then Jesus, in the middle of their laughter, drops the ultimate bomb.

Verse 27: *"And the lord of that slave felt compassion and released him and forgave him the debt."*

"I forgive you...You owe me no debt!" Joyous response erupts from the crowd. Their emotions are wearing out by now; laughter, tears..., and now—what a celebration! Unbelievable relief comes over them. The King forgives the slave; he owes Him no debt! This is unheard of; no one has ever done that before.

But Jesus isn't finished yet. As the celebration calms down and the dust settles, Jesus says

Verse 28: *"But the slave went out and found one of his fellow slaves who owed him a hundred denarii; and he seized him and began to choke him, saying,*

'Pay back what you owe.'"

The slave did what? He found a guy who owed him a day's wage, seized upon him and began choking him! Why would anyone do that? Why would anyone who has just been completely forgiven $10,000,000 choke someone who owes him one day's wages? What is he thinking?

Think about how out of character this response is. If you or I were forgiven $10,000,000 we'd be screaming and jumping up and down celebrating. We would be crying and finding everyone we could to announce the glorious news. We would even call a news conference and inform the media. We've been forgiven the national debt!

This shows just how much the King of the universe desires a relationship with His creation. The One who spoke the worlds into existence, who reigns in the glory-flashing, rainbow-encircled covenant throne of God, desires relationship with you. Jesus knew that the only way He could secure that relationship was to settle the insurmountable debt that existed between you and Him. He knew you couldn't pay this debt, and though He didn't owe it, He paid it for you out of love.

By the way, your credit card company doesn't want you to settle your debt. Have you realized this yet? They want you to owe, because as long as you do, they control some part of your life. They like to keep you owing so you keep on paying. As long as you owe, they own.

Jesus Desires a Debt-Free Relationship

Jesus knows that debt is a detriment to fellowship. If I owe you and can't pay you, I would rather not meet you in the store. I'm guilty, I'm condemned, I'm ashamed, and I'm embarrassed. I owe you and I can't pay. I'll probably not invite you to have coffee this week. I can't pay, so I'm uncomfortable in your presence. I don't even answer your calls.

God knew this mountain of debt would quickly become a wall of division because our debt to Him was insurmountable. We could not pay, so in His presence we became uncomfortable, guilty, condemned, and ashamed. God despised that, so He came in the person of Jesus—God stood up from the throne and moved to do something about the debt.

We connect the spiritual equation here. Christ forgave us an insurmountable debt at Calvary. He released us by hanging on that cross with the blood of God pouring out for our redemption. He came into the market place where we were held for ransom. He brought with Him the purchase price – the blood of God. He took us off the market at Calvary by satisfying our debt with God and thus destroyed the works of the devil. That's redemption.

We see that. We can even appreciate it to some degree. However, what about this slave in the parable choking the one who owed him? What's his deal? He's religious. Like most religious people, he only heard his own voice. He was talking so loud that he failed to hear Christ say, *"You owe me no debt."* All he could hear were his own words, *"Give me time, I will repay."* It's the only way you can explain his ridiculous actions.

The slave was forgiven an enormous debt, yet he began choking the first person he could find to get a payment. What was he doing? DEBT COLLECTING. **He didn't realize he had been given forgiveness, he thought he had been given time.** Please read that profound statement again. He didn't realize he had been forgiven ; he thought he had been given time to pay back his debt. Evidently he wasn't about to waste a second—choke the first poor guy you find.

The Layaway Plan

I call this credit card religion. Many Christians think they're going to heaven on the layaway plan—pay a little at a time. They haven't heard Christ say, *"You owe me no debt. You are completely forgiven. Forever!"* They only hear their own religious rhetoric.

Does this sound like anything or anyone you know? It should, it's a picture of religion and the religious. It's the reason some Christians strive, work, sweat, and fear. It's the reason they use others and insult, judge, and condemn. It's the reason there's so much religious elbowing in the Body of Christ, and so much competition and religious garbage.

Too many Christians can't believe they're really forgiven. If they don't believe it and don't receive it, then they have to try to collect it. Of course, they're going to collect it from you. They'll demand of your marriage, your friends, your job, your church, and your relationships what only a healthy relationship with Christ can give. They would like to have a relationship with Him, but they owe. They're not comfortable. They're ashamed and afraid, so they're not returning His calls.

All the while Jesus is saying, *"You owe me no debt. Why don't you allow me in your life? I don't come to condemn you, or to hurt or embarrass you. I've come to love you. 'For God did not send the Son into the world to judge the world, but that the world should be saved through Him'"* (John 3:17).

Why don't we hear that? Why don't we stop suffocating every relationship and stop running from marriage to marriage, job to job, and city to city demanding what's already been paid? Let's stop collecting and just relax and rejoice in it. Let's open the door and fellowship with the One who forgave us. He paid the debt; there is nothing left to pay.

A Prayer

Verse 34: *"And his lord, moved with anger handed him over to the torturers until he should repay all that was owed him."*

This is the reason so many people live miserable, tormented lives, even many Christians. They have not heard the King say, "You owe me no debt." Striving and working, sweating and grabbing, they live under the tormenting fear of not being able to pay. They're religious, and it's torture.

Hear what the King says: *"You owe me no debt."* Believe what the King says and be at peace. I speak a prayer of life over you. I command torment, striving, and religious struggling to leave you now. Be free in the freedom in which Christ has made you free. In Jesus' mighty name…Amen!

Remember these key points:

1. **Reject Religion—Embrace the People**

    When you receive Jesus Christ, He puts His love in your heart for all people. God loves the world, and not only in a general sense—He loves each and every person individually. Furthermore, God leads you to love and receive every person in *His* love and acceptance.

2. **Paul's Heart's Desire**

    This Jew of all Jews had a heavy heart concerning his brethren (the Jews). He not only prayed for their salvation but went to them first. Time after time in city after city, Paul preached Jesus Christ to them and this revelation of grace. Although individual Jews received his message and his Christ, as a nation his brethren rejected him and severely persecuted him. However, their treatment of him never stopped his continual prayer for them in regard to their salvation.

3. **Three Shortcomings of the Jewish Religion**

    Shortcoming #1: They didn't know about Jesus righteousness.

    Shortcoming #2: They sought to establish their own righteousness.

    Shortcoming #3: They did not subject themselves to the righteousness of God.

4. **The Debt Collector**

    Refusing to accept the great gift of salvation purchased by Jesus Christ at Calvary as sufficient causes you to go through life striving to pay a debt which has already been paid.

5. **Jesus Desires a Debt-Free Relationship**

    God knew this mountain of debt would quickly become a wall of division because our debt to Him was insurmountable. We could not pay, so in His presence we became uncomfortable, guilty, condemned, and ashamed. God despised that, so He came in the person of Jesus—God stood up from the throne and moved to do something about the debt.

6. **The Layaway Plan**

    I call this credit card religion. Many Christians think they're going to heaven on the layaway plan; pay a little at a time. They haven't heard Christ say,

"You owe me no debt. You are completely forgiven. Forever!" They only hear their own religious rhetoric.

7. **A Prayer**

    Hear what the King says, *"You owe me no debt."* Believe what the King says and be at peace. I speak a prayer of life over you. I command torment, striving, and religious struggling to leave you now. Be free in the freedom in which Christ has made you free. In Jesus' mighty name I pray. Amen!

Chapter 6

It's Really Very Simple

I tried to read his eyes across the table in the restaurant. I knew he was a good man, but I sensed his mixed emotions. Was he going to try again? Could he trust one more time? Was there really any sanity in this church thing? Was there any preacher truly interested in his concerns?

The conversation between our wives helped relieve some of the tension at the table. His wife had been attending our church for a few weeks now, and though she was still confused and injured, she wanted her husband to meet Sandra and me and give our church a try. She was willing; would he give church a try just one more time?

Words can't express what this precious family had experienced over the years in search of truth in the church. The destruction, legalism, judgment, and bondage had taken a toll on them as they searched for an intimate relationship with Christ. I sensed their deep love for Jesus, but at the same time felt the deep pain that people had inflicted on them. Nevertheless, here they were. Their love for God and their true relationship with Him was compelling them to reach out one more time. Would they open their trust again, here, now? Would they ever find a safe place to grow and mature in the true accepting love of God, or would life be better just loving God and finding Him in their own personal private devotions?

It's Elementary

We've already discussed how difficult Hebrews is to understand without the proper tools. Now we come to what could arguably be among the most difficult passages in the Epistle:

> *Therefore leaving the elementary teaching about the Christ, let us press on to maturity, not laying again a foundation of repentance from dead works and of faith toward God, of instruction about washings, and laying on of hands, and the resurrection of the dead, and eternal judgment.*
>
> (Hebrews 6:1-2)

The writer admonishes his audience to go on to something else and to leave what he calls *"the elementary teaching about the Christ,"* which he enumerates as:

- Laying again the foundation of repentance from dead works
- Faith toward God
- Instructions about washings
- Laying on of hands
- The resurrection
- Eternal judgment

On the surface, this list sounds much like a list of New Testament, New Covenant principles. However, there is an evident red flag, which invites us to inquire deeper into its nature. This red flag is a principle stated in verse 2, an "instruction about washings," undoubtedly an Old Covenant or Old Testament teaching.

Let's re-examine the entire list and look at these principles in verses 1 and 2. Since we're instructed to leave or abandon them and to go on to something else, it's vital that we clearly understand what we should abandon and what we should go on to embrace.

Go on to Maturity in What?[1]

You may have heard teachers say that "going on to maturity" means we should mature beyond these elementary teachings. However, a problem arises when we identify this list with New Testament principles **because they aren't**. The New Testament writers would never urge us to leave or abandon fundamental, foundational truths, nor would they instruct us to leave any New Covenant teachings of Jesus Christ: repentance, laying on of hands, or truths about the resurrection. These truths are fundamental to our faith and must never be abandoned! They must be embraced, and continually taught and practiced. These are the basic truths of the Great Commission woven inseparably into the fabric of the New Testament.

The force of the terminology in the Greek that communicates the writer's admonition "to leave" and "to go on," makes this subject even more critical. The Greek word *aphiemi* translated as "leaving" means, "to put or place," "off" or "away." The basic idea of the verb is of an action which causes separation.

---

[1] Some material from this section is derived from Kenneth Wuest's *Volume II Word Studies in the Greek New Testament*, Grand Rapids: Eerdmans, 1947.

Other uses of the word include "to let go," "to disregard," or "to send away." Alford explains it as

Leaving as behind and done with in order to go on to another thing.

Now the desire of the writer becomes clear—he wants these Hebrews to be done with, separated from, and detached from what he has presented in the list. However, you must understand that no teacher would encourage New Covenant believers to disregard these vital fundamental truths if they were truly New Covenant teachings.

We now come to the Greek word *phero*, which is translated "let us go on." This word means "to carry along" or "to bear along." The writer of this Epistle is urging these hearers to abandon and disregard one thing so they can be carried along to something greater. This is much like what he did in chapters 11 and 12 where he urged them to leave behind the past heroes of faith, over whom they stumbled, and to *"fix their eyes on Jesus the author and finisher of faith."*

It's evident that the writer is not advising the readers to abandon a list of vital New Testament principles. Rather, he is admonishing them to leave, abandon, and totally disregard a list of Old Covenant principles that will cause them to stumble and prevent them from going on. Leaving these First Testament teachings enables them to be carried along to Perfection, the Lord Jesus Christ Himself. They are not admonished to go on to "maturity" as in some translations, but "unto perfection" (KJV). Something that is yet unborn cannot mature. These Hebrews have not yet been born in Christ; therefore, they cannot mature. However, they are urged to go on to perfection, and perfection is a Person—Jesus Christ. It's in Christ that they will find the total fulfillment and satisfaction of all the Old Covenant symbolism.

The red flag instruction about washings properly warned us. The writer admonished his readers to disregard Old Testament baggage that would lead them back to animal sacrifice and an ultimate severance from Christ. If they were to go back, they would commit the blasphemous, unpardonable sin of Hebrews 10:29, and would receive the severe punishment that accompanies…

- trampling under foot the Son of God
- regarding as unclean the blood of the Covenant
- insulting the Spirit of Grace

The Principles Defined

The principles in Hebrews 6:1-2 represent old Law principles that begin with the following:

✓ **Repentance from dead works** [2]

Dead works are just that—DEAD. No matter what you do to or with them, they will not produce life. They are dead. Looking at the list the writer identifies in verses 1 and 2, one can readily see that it is comprised mainly of the dead works from which these Hebrews should repent or turn away. One cannot relate to dead works as if they were alive or produced life, they must be put away and abandoned instead. The writer was, in essence, saying: "Don't be hindered in your forward progress by dragging something dead into your future." Repentance from dead works means repentance toward God.

---

[2] The original concept of this teaching is borrowed from Wuest's *Volume II Word Studies in the Greek New Testament*, p112

✓ **Faith toward God**

The Old Testament teaching of faith toward God is sharply contrasted to the New Testament teaching of faith in our Lord Jesus Christ. Once Christ came, our view is no longer looking forward as if expecting Him. He has come. He lives in us, and our faith must not stretch *toward* Him as if He were distant, but *in* Him because He inhabits believers.

✓ **The doctrine of washings**

This was our red flag principle that caused us to re-examine the list. This Old Testament teaching refers to the ceremonial ablutions or washings of Judaism which have no place in our New Covenant faith.

✓ **Laying on of hands** [3]

This principle refers to the transferral of sin from the Levitical priest to the scapegoat. This activity typifies the removal of sin from Israel, and speaks of the coming "Azazel," Christ Himself. This is a great teaching, but it's *dead*. With the arrival of the true Azazel, the time has come to move from faith *toward* God and to embrace faith in the One to whom this great teaching points—**the Lord Jesus Christ.** Now that the True Life has come, the continual rehearsal of the prophecy without receiving its promise results in dead works.

✓ **Resurrection of the dead**

This Old Testament teaching is a dead principle when absent from its total development in the New Testament. Instead, we look to the One who has now come, the Resurrection Himself.

---

[3] This is not to be confused with the Laying on of hands taught in other New Testament Scriptures.

✓ **Eternal judgment**

This teaching in the old dispensation excludes the New Testament concept of "no judgment" for the believer in Messiah. The New Testament believer does not receive judgment but has passed from death unto life. Furthermore, without the Righteous Judge, true judgment does not exist.

The writer implores his readers that Christ is better. Because Christ is better, don't return to these Old Testament teachings. Put them away. They are dead. Disregard and be separated from what hinders and go on to faith in the New Testament sacrifice, the Lamb of God, Jesus Christ.

The writer of Hebrews has admonished these readers from the beginning not to go back to the animal sacrifices and to no longer count animal blood important as related to the blood of the precious Lamb of God, Jesus Christ. Now he warns of the danger of embracing *anything* that would trip them causing them to turn in the wrong direction, putting their focus on the blood of animals and not on the blood of Jesus.

This insight is important for us today. It is dangerous to embrace old Law ceremony or old Law principles and instructions as if they would bring us to a better relationship or deeper maturity in Christ. Hebrews teaches us not to offer animal sacrifice, which is blasphemy and would sever us from Christ. We're also taught to send away and abandon any idea, teaching, or tendency that would have us embrace any fragment of Old Testament dogma. Embracing these teachings only serves to turn our eyes backward and bring a stumbling block to our walk with Christ.

Hebrews sounds the clearest call to the New Testament church to leave behind and be done with, to separate from, or send away and disregard all the principles that are not of the New

Covenant. The writer urges us to leave them and go forward into the New Covenant truths and the blessings of Christ and His grace.

Falling Away

For in the case of those who have once been enlightened and have tasted of the heavenly gift and have been made partakers of the Holy Spirit, and have tasted the good word of God and the powers of the age to come, and then have fallen away, it is impossible to renew them again to repentance since they again crucify to themselves the Son of God, and put Him open to shame.

(Hebrews 6:4-6)

We stumble over these verses in our attempts to make them fit our New Testament theology. They do fit, but not apart from the keys of understanding Hebrews that safely lead us into the harbor of truth. Much time could be spent wrangling about the words used in verses 4 and 5 and whether or not they refer to New Testament believers. Arguments can be made that these verses only apply to the Hebrews who had only mentally assented to the gospel and not mixed the truth with faith and received Christ in their hearts.

However, whether these verses refer to believers or non-believers is not the most vital key in understanding these verses. The key is in the first line of verse 6 *"...and then have fallen away."* Before we identify who is falling away, lets identify the meaning of "fall away."

To "fall away" in the context of this Epistle is to do what is described in Hebrews 10:29—to turn away from the precious blood of Jesus, which is the power and cleansing for our salvation, and to turn back to the blood of bulls and goats. To do this is to

- trample under foot the Son of God
- regard as unclean the blood of the covenant
- insult the Spirit of Grace

This is blasphemy! This would sever a person from Christ. No matter where a person is today in his or her walk with God (whether just mentally assenting or totally redeemed), "to fall away" is to embrace the anti-Christian blasphemy of animal sacrifice *"after coming to the knowledge of the truth."* Anyone who has heard the Gospel of Jesus Christ inclusive of the truth of His precious blood atonement and then obstinately offers the blood of bulls and goats has fallen away. Only in this extreme and blasphemous condition is one severed from Christ.

Innocent Beginnings

Nearly all destroyed relationships start with rather innocent beginnings. Innumerable stories emerge from marriage counseling sessions where a broken and weeping husband talks of the first glance toward that "other woman." He tells how that glance turned into a sensual look and then into passionate desire.

How many times has the pastor or counselor heard: "She understood me. I felt I could really open up to her." What began as casual conversation turned into secret phone calls, private dinner dates, and ultimately a motel rendezvous. The subtle trap set by the devil results in the tragic loss of marriage, family, respect, and integrity, not to mention a lost testimony.

Likewise is the road back into legalistic bondage for the Christian. The flesh entertains some law attitude that is seemingly innocent enough. Nevertheless, over time, this judgmental carnality begins to turn the believer's focus back to external legalism and to embracing of principles that cause him or her to stumble in their relationship with Christ.

Again the door is open for striving, jealousy, greed and every fleshly evil work. The chamber inside the believer, once cleansed and set apart for God's anointing, gifting, and worship, becomes cluttered with a legalism that moves in to dominate and control. The attitudes that were once flowing from the Tree of Life return to the Tree of Knowledge of Good and Evil.

External religious criterion suffocates your relationship with Christ and sends your Christianity into a struggling wilderness experience. You awaken one day and realize that what began as a joyful celebration of love and life in Christ, has now become a lumbering, striving, wearisome drudgery as you plod through ankle-deep wilderness sand. The fresh breezes of Holy Spirit deliverance and excitement have been overwhelmed by the heavy weight of Law Commandments and external judgment that bear down on your shoulders like a seventy-pound backpack.

Other Externals

While we're talking about external criteria and Levitical Law works, let's not fail to point out the quagmire of other religious legalism that can just as quickly hinder your grace walk in Christ. Many Christians will never have to deal directly with a Levitical system—Law works argument bellowed from some Judaizing Gentile dressed up like a rabbi with his shofar drawn and ready. Nevertheless, all Christians must continually be aware of the strong flesh-pull, enticing them back to any brand of religious legalism.

Religious arguments regarding the length of one's hair, jewelry, social status, financial status, and clothing styles have repeatedly created church splits and have even formed new denominations. The lengthy and embarrassing list of ridiculous religious criteria weighs down on many precious believers. Religion trips them and causes them to stumble in their pursuit of the heart of God. Because they're hungry for God, they listen and obey legalistic teachers.

If you've been around the church for any significant amount of time, you've either encountered this religious brainwash or you've heard the horrific stories. Some members of my church came from a place where the brand of tennis shoes they wore was external criteria related to holiness and spiritual maturity. Thank God they're delivered and healed today and serve as anointed leaders in the church. But by their own testimony, they were giving up on organized religion. They loved Christ, but the joy of their salvation was buried under the debris of external legalism.

The Pentecostal movement lost nearly an entire generation a few decades ago because of its hard-line religious rules against roller skating, bowling, ball games, and movies. I know some wonderful older people today who had to give up athletic scholarships to college and careers in professional sports because of the rules of their church.

Many who have come back to the church still battle bitterness. Others have never even turned back to look at the church because of suffocating external criteria and religious judgment poured on what began as a sensitive relationship with Christ.

I believe I'm safe in saying that every Sunday morning in America, there are more Christians at home sleeping than attending church. These are born again people with their name written in the Book of Life but injured by the heavy weight of religious judgment and condemnation. Tragically, unlike the couple in the story at the beginning of the chapter, they refuse to give the church another try. For sure, they are being ripped off from a wealth of faith and joy in Christ, but more tragically, their children are kept away from Sunday school and the precious principles of Christ taught in the church. Sadly, these people can't trust that there could be a truly safe place for their faith.

Worse is a nation and world filled with lost and hurting people who never have experienced Christ and possibly never will. You know them. They say they hate God and refuse to talk about "religion," ridiculing you when you do. They are so hard, you can't even get close with your love for them and your Christian testimony.

Understand this: It's not because of you. In fact, if the truth were known they really don't hate God. How can they hate someone they don't even know? Anyone who knows God loves Him. They don't hate God, they hate the people who came to them representing Him. They hate those condescending, Bible-thumping, judgmental, criticizing religionists who have come to them pointing fingers of accusation. If they could ever get over what those people have done to them, they would listen to your message of love and joy in Christ. But don't give up. Continue to pray. Remember, God found you, so you keep loving and being there for them. The love of Christ will reach them through you.

Set the People Free!

Too many pastors and Bible teachers have either been taught or have assumed for themselves that they have a mandate to keep people bound by legalism. They see it as their responsibility to keep members in line lest they run wild in some carnal, hedonistic flesh revolution.

Leaders, I challenge you with this mandate: **Set God's people free!** Tell them how much Jesus loves them and how He will never leave nor forsake them. Help people dig out from under the burdensome lie of religious judgment, because when they do, they will discover that the New Testament church is real and it's alive.

This righteous church is made up of a people who love God. They have a proper New Testament perspective that trusts the Christ in them to bring them into His righteousness. They are people with a pure heart who are ready to be disciplined in the ways of God.

If you are a pastor, you will find it a delight to pastor a church like this. You'll discover really neat people in your church, and then more will start showing up. You'll discover that people who are free from judgment don't judge. That people healed of their wounds don't wound. That people who are blessed and forgiven, bless and forgive. The joy of your church and the excitement of love and acceptance will return, and you'll discover something quite remarkable: A new delight in your ministry. Then, you'll write me and say thanks.

Here's the mission statement of the church Sandra and I founded eighteen years ago:

> *The Kingdom of God is a nonjudgmental society that speaks dignity and esteem to every person that we meet. Jesus accepts you right where you are and so do we. You do not have to pass a religious exam to be welcome here. Just come and be ready to receive your brothers and sisters in Christ right where they*

are. Jesus accepts us right where we are and loves us there. We have no right to be any other way.

New Life Christian Fellowship is a growing, dynamic, interdenominational, interracial family of excited and righteous believers who constantly live in the state of revival. I'm in love with them and they're in love with me, and you can feel the love when you walk in.

The New Testament church really has a relevant message. You'll discover that message under the garbage heap of external criteria and judgmental religion that is suffocating it. Let's get a Holy Spirit rake and uncover this relevant church so that it can be revealed to a dying humanity. There is a hungry world out there that is ready for the true Gospel. Jesus is still the answer for the world today!

Don't go back! This message is just as relevant today as it was 2,000 years ago. Don't go back into a lifestyle that destroys. Embrace the grace of Jesus Christ and the power of the Holy Spirit and you will live in the presence of the One who accepts

---

Remember these key points:

1. **Go Beyond What's Elementary.**

   We must abandon *"the elementary teaching about the Christ"* and go on to something else—perfection

2. **Go on to Maturity in What?**

   What is yet unborn cannot mature. These Hebrews had not yet been born in Christ; therefore they couldn't mature. They are urged to go on to perfection, and that perfection is a Person—Jesus Christ. Only in Christ will they find the total fulfillment and satisfaction of all the Old Covenant symbolism.

you—all of you.

3. **The Principles Defined as Elementary Are:**
   - ✓ Repentance from dead works
   - ✓ Faith toward God
   - ✓ The doctrine of washings
   - ✓ Laying on of hands
   - ✓ Resurrection of the dead
   - ✓ Eternal judgment

4. **Keep from Falling Away**

   To "fall away" in the context of this Epistle is to turn away from the precious blood of Jesus, which is the power and cleansing for our salvation, and to turn back to the blood of bulls and goats.

5. **Innocent Beginnings Can Be Suffocated by Religion**

   External religious criteria suffocate your relationship with Christ and sends your Christianity into a struggling wilderness experience. One day you realize that what began as a joyful celebration of love and life in Christ has become a lumbering, striving, wearisome drudgery as you plod through ankle-deep wilderness sand. The fresh breeze of Holy Spirit deliverance and excitement has been overwhelmed by the heavy weight of law commandments and external judgment that bears down on your shoulders like a seventy-pound backpack.

6. **Don't Be Weighed Down by Externals**

   Religious arguments regarding the length of hair, jewelry, social status, financial status, and clothing styles have repeatedly created church splits and have even formed new denominations. Religion trips believers and causes them to stumble in their pursuit of the heart of God.

7. **Set the People Free!**

Leaders, I challenge you with this mandate: **Set God's people free!** Tell them how much Jesus loves them and how He will never leave them nor forsake them. Help people dig out from under the burdensome lie of religious judgment, because when they do, they will find the New Testament church is real and alive.

Chapter 7

Don't Go Back!

Serena was astonished. How could Nancy even think of going out with Ron again? He had been mean to her. He had cheated on her. Nothing she had ever done had garnered even the slightest bit of respect from him. What was she doing?

"Nancy. How can you let him convince you to go out again? You know that he's just looking for an easy date."

"No he's not," said Nancy. "He really cares for me. He told me so."

What Nancy didn't know was that Ron was seeing someone else. They'd had an argument and he was showing her that he still had a few options open. He'd show her a lesson.

"Nancy. He's dating Maria. I saw them together last week. Don't you see? He's using you."

"I'm going out with him, Serena. I know my Ron. He really means it this time."

Sadly, Nancy was devastated again. She was so badly scarred from her relationship with Ron that she refused any contact with men and turned to other women to satisfy her need for love. Too bad she didn't listen. Too bad she went back.

Jewish Roots

A few years ago my wife Sandra and I, along with some special friends, took our second trip to Israel. We based our tour out of Tiberius on the shore of the sea of Galilee. Our hotel sat on a hill above the city from which we could see Galilee and the Golan Heights. Each morning we would awake and look out across the valley and behold the beautiful view that rose above the sea on the far side. Powerful thoughts filled my mind as I viewed such rich beauty and pondered such holy history! I have a picture in my office of Sandra and me standing on the side of the hill where Christ preached His Sermon on the Mount. The fog lifting in the scene is almost as surreal as our memories of the trip.

One day, Sandra and I stayed behind in Tiberius while our tour group went to visit some other sites. We'll never forget the baskets of fish, still alive and flopping around, as they poured out onto the sidewalks of this area where Jesus and His disciples spent so much time. We bless that land. We bless Israel and pray for her people. However, as a Gentile, that's as far back as I can go.

Jews have Jewish roots. These roots relate them by blood to Moses, Abraham, Isaac, Joseph, David, and even Matthew, Mark, Paul and Peter. When it comes to roots, tradition and history, Jews are most enriched. They have Moses, the Ten Commandments, the patriarchs, the Torah, the Menorah, the temple, the shofar. They have the Seder and the Sabbath. Furthermore, the Jews have the Holy Land!

Gentiles don't have Jewish roots. The Holy Land isn't ours; we only visit. We're tourists there, so we buy souvenirs of olive wood and gifts and bring them back home. Israel is not our home; it is Jewish roots. The Jews are great friends and allies and we love them, but our roots are in the United States.

Coal Miner Roots

I was born in the South, the son of a preacher. At an early age my family moved to the Midwest and then to the Northeast. Later in my teens, we moved to Florida where I met my beautiful wife and where now, many years later, we live and pastor.

I've never lived in West Virginia. However, both of my grandfathers lived and worked there. They both retired from #9 Coal Mine up the hollow in Cabin Creek, some miles outside of Charleston. My dad worked with his dad in the mine until he was twenty-five years old, then he received Christ and was called into the ministry.

My dad had been diagnosed with tuberculosis when he received Christ. I still remember him telling me the story about the night of his salvation. He told about the building where the revival meeting was held, and how there was sawdust on the floor. When the salvation call was made, he went forward and spent two hours in the sawdust with God. It ruined his new suit, but he stood up saved and totally healed!

As I write this, my dad is in his mid 80s, and he and my mother have been married for fifty-nine years, fifty-seven of which were spent in the ministry. He's still plugged in. In fact, he works with me on staff at our local church. I'm proud of my heritage and of my coal miner roots of West Virginia.

Nothing Remains the Same

A few years ago, we all went back—my mom and dad, my brother and his wife, my wife, Sandra and me. I hadn't been back in forty years, but I still had memories. Oh the memories.

I remember my granddad Linkous coming home from the coal mine, his face blackened by coal dust except where his helmet covered his head. After washing off the grime of a day's work, he and I would walk up the tracks to the company store where he would buy something for me. When we returned home, he would sit on the porch with his friends where they would tell stories, whittle, and chew and spit tobacco till dark.

I'll never forget those memories—the smell of the coal fireplace and my grandma cooking that delicious West Virginia ham.

You really can't go back because nothing remains the same back there. Not only is the house gone, but the bridge across the creek that took us to the house is gone as well. The company store was demolished—we had to guess where it used to be. It hurt me that everything had disappeared and nothing was like I remembered it to be forty years earlier.

I parked where the bridge used to be and got out of the van. My emotions were in turmoil, I needed to be alone. Trying to unravel my thoughts, I walked toward the creek away from everyone else. Everything was gone, and I felt anger toward who tore it all down. Nothing was the same.

The pain I felt for Dad and Mom was especially acute. Nothing was left to identify our past, our heritage or our roots. As I bent over to gather up some small pieces of coal to take back to the van, uncontrollable tears from a pool of emotions deep within began to fill my eyes. It embarrassed me to be crying, so I did my best to hide the tears. Then I felt a hand on my shoulder, and

I looked up to see that Sandra, my beautiful, understanding and loving wife was standing with me.

Regaining my composure, I brought the pieces of coal back to the van. When I handed it to my dad, I was surprised to see that they were all crying as well. For whatever reason, we all had a good cry. It was a bonding, cleansing cry, the kind that seems to wash away old wounds and sets one free to move on, to live, to laugh, and to love.

I hugged my gray-haired dad and kissed him on his head. Then I started the van and we drove away. Cabin Creek was framed in our rear view mirror and in our memories forever.

Today those pieces of coal are in my study at home. Along with the coal are some pictures of Cabin Creek, a book about Kanawa County, West Virginia, some carvings made out of coal, and items from the mines similar to what my dad had used. I especially like the carbon lanterns they wore on their miner's helmets to light the miles of darkness underground. I still sit spellbound as my dad tells those coal miner stories about him and his dad. How they would enter in the pre-dawn hours and emerge after dark, and how they would lie on their bellies in a thirty-inch high shaft and ride three miles into the mountain on a little car on rails.

Level Ground

Forgive me if I dwell on these personal memories, but I do it to illustrate my roots. These are my roots. I am a Gentile, so I don't have Jewish roots.

Paul wrote:

> *Therefore remember, that formerly you, the Gentiles*

> *in the flesh, who are called "Uncircumcision" by the so-called "Circumcision" which is performed in the flesh by human hands—*
>
> *remember that you were at that time separate from Christ, excluded from the commonwealth of Israel, and strangers to the covenants of promise, having no hope and without God in the world.*
>
> (Ephesians 2:11-12)

As Gentiles, we don't have deep treasures in Jewish roots. We were separate from Christ and strangers to the covenants. We had no hope and were without God. However, the Good News comes in the following verses:

> *But now in Christ Jesus you who formerly were far off have been brought near by the blood of Christ.*
>
> *For He Himself is our peace, who made both groups into one, and broke down the barrier of the dividing wall,*
>
> *by abolishing in His flesh the enmity, which is the Law of commandments contained in ordinances, that in Himself He might make the two into one new man, thus establishing peace,*
>
> *and might reconcile them both in one body to God through the cross, by it having put to death the enmity.*
>
> *And He came and preached peace to you who were far away, and preached to those who were near;*
>
> *for through Him we both have our access in one Spirit to the Father.*
>
> (Ephesians 2:13-18)

Hallelujah! This is the message of the Gospel. No matter how lost you were, no matter how separated you were, you have been made near by the BLOOD OF CHRIST!

It doesn't matter about roots! The ground is level at the foot of the Cross. Christ leveled it and took away every advantage, except in Him, that anyone assumed they had. It doesn't matter how deep or shallow your roots, because they mean nothing! Only Christ means something. Christ means everything.

Paul declared that the Gentiles who had nothing and the Jews who had something became equal at the foot of the Cross. But don't be confused. Pay careful attention to this: Christ didn't level the ground by giving the Gentiles Jewish roots. He leveled the ground by abolishing Jewish roots in reference to their spiritual value. He abolished or rendered inoperative the enmity, which is the Law of Commandments and the ordinances that had given them advantage.

If bringing something to the Cross could have brought an advantage, the Jews would have done it. However, Christ broke down any advantage that would divide us by abolishing anything that gave a head start. The Jews' Law of commandments, ceremonies and patriarchs mean nothing when it comes to relationship with Christ. He takes everyone's advantage away, and we all start over at the same place. That place is Jesus.

The Great Exchange

You bring nothing when you come to Christ, yet He gives you His everything. The Cross is the great exchange! At the Cross, Christ took your

- darkness and gave you His light
- sin and gave you His righteousness

- disease and gave you His healing
- hell and gave you His heaven
- death and gave you His life

What did I bring to the exchange? Just my broken, repentant self. I had nothing to give for such a marvelous gift He offered.

This is where you must come for salvation. If you think you have an advantage because you are a Jew, or because you are from West Virginia, or because of your social status, or because of your financial position, or because of your education, think again. These are nothing compared to the great gift of Calvary. Jesus Christ abolished any advantage, and He allows nothing to compete with Him and His salvation.

> *For by grace you have been saved through faith; and that not of yourselves, it is the gift of God;*
>
> *not as a result of works, that no one should boast.*
>
> *For we are His workmanship, created in Christ Jesus for good works, which God prepared beforehand, that we should walk in them.*
>
> (Ephesians 2:8-10)

Any advantage would have to be external, legalistic, man-made criteria that would destroy the innocence and simplicity of God's great gift of salvation in Christ. No one brings advantage to this exchange.

The Religion of Cain

The attitude of Cain demonstrates an advantage mentality. Cain liked what he brought for sacrifice and he wouldn't put it down. It was lovely and valuable. He had worked hard over it and wanted it recognized. However, God said it meant nothing. Bring a lamb. God didn't want what was valuable to Cain; God wanted what was valuable to Him—an obedient, humble, repentant heart (Genesis 4:1-7).

Scripture says that the Law produces wrath (Romans 4:15). Law works produce wrath because they expect and demand recognition. Works compete *with* God *for* God's glory. However, in comparison to God's gift of salvation, His love, and His holiness, everything we have is worthless! Therefore, we bring our nothing, yet receive His everything. He is our righteousness. Cain's wrath ultimately resulted in the murder of his brother Abel, just as the Pharisees' wrath murdered Christ. Jesus wouldn't accept or condone their works as worthy and honorable, so they killed Him.

It is ridiculous and heretical to add external works to your salvation in an attempt to deepen your relationship with Christ. Menorahs, prayer shawls, observing the Sabbath, feast days, or circumcision rites add absolutely nothing to your relationship with Christ.

It would be no more ridiculous for me to reach back to my West Virginia roots and claim that something there makes me holier and closer to God, than it would be for a Jew or Judaizing Gentile to teach that something from Jewish roots will give an advantage in one's relationship with Christ.

How ridiculous it would be for me to tell you to take pilgrimages to Cabin Creek or invest in a carbide lantern to burn during your prayers while you chew tobacco and whittle so you can be closer to God. No more ridiculous than for someone to claim that you need a prayer shawl, a menorah or a shofar to enhance your relationship to Christ or to call you to worship.

This kind of heretical teaching is diametrically opposed to the Gospel of Jesus Christ. These heresies proliferate on creating external criteria that runs back to legalistic bondage and Law works ceremonialism. They move your personal relationship with Christ away from an internal work of Holy Spirit indwelling to the external works ethic of Judaizing legalism. Paul says that if anyone comes preaching any other gospel, that person is condemned (Galatians 1:6-9).

We can all enjoy and embrace our roots and share the personal values of our past. Many of these things can be enjoyed as personal memories or even national tradition, but none of these add anything to our continuing and deepening relationship to and in Christ. God makes sure of it. Paul makes it clear in Ephesians 2 that no one has a condescending advantage. Christ levels the ground at the cross. We all come empty handed, broken and contrite and begin there, in Christ alone.

There Is Neither Jew Nor Gentile

Flesh runs back to Law works because it loves the external criteria. The person in charge of the criteria becomes the judge, who gets to say who's in and who's out, who's holy and who's not, who's worthy, who's spiritual... the list goes on and on. For this reason, God doesn't allow that foolishness in the New Testament mentality. *Christ in you* provides the only hope of glory and the only avenue to spiritual maturity.

Put away confusion, put away deceit, and don't allow your fleshly desires to run you back to religious foolishness and sin. You *were* married to the Law, but *now* you are married to Christ (Romans 7:6). Christ is better. Don't go back.

> *For as many as are of the works of the Law are under a curse; for it is written, "Cursed is everyone who does not abide by all things written in the book of the*

law, to perform them."

Now that no one is justified by the Law before God is evident; for, "The righteous man shall live by faith."

However, the Law is not of faith; on the contrary, "He who practices them shall live by them."

Christ redeemed us from the curse of the Law, having become a curse for us—for is written—"Cursed is everyone who hangs on a tree"—

in order that in Christ Jesus the blessing of Abraham might come to the Gentiles, so that we might receive the promise of the Spirit through faith.
(Galatians 3:10-14)

Therefore the Law has become our tutor to lead us to Christ, that we may be justified by faith.

But now that faith has come, we are no longer under a tutor.

For you are all sons of God through faith in Christ Jesus.

For all of you who were baptized into Christ have clothed yourself with Christ.

There is neither Jew nor Greek*, there is neither male nor female; for you are all one in Christ Jesus.*
(Galatians 3: 24-28)

There is neither Jew nor Greek. Can the Scripture be more clear? One has to be very confused and deceived to go back. The only place to go is forward into Christ, and Christ has leveled the ground. *"Nevertheless knowing that a man is not justified by the works of the Law but through faith in Christ Jesus, even we have believed in Christ Jesus, that we may be justified by faith in Christ, and not by the works of the Law; since by the works of the Law shall no flesh be justified"* (Galatians 2:16).

Severed from Christ

The letter to the Hebrews was addressed to a group of individuals in the First Century Church (specifically Hebrews) who had heard the gospel. They had mentally assented to it, but had not mixed the message with faith and received Christ in their hearts as Savior. Now, they were under great persecution and on the verge of going back to temple worship and animal sacrifice.

However, the Epistle to the Galatians was written as a general letter to all the churches in the region of Galatia. It was written because Judaizers were frustrating the peace in these churches and attacking Paul's message of grace and salvation in Christ alone. Paul wrote:

> *It was for freedom that Christ set us free; therefore keep standing firm and do not be subject again to a yoke of slavery.*
>
> *Behold I, Paul, say to you that if you receive circumcision, Christ will be of no benefit to you.*
>
> *And I testify again to every man who receives circumcision, that he is under obligation to keep the whole Law.*
>
> ***You have been severed from Christ,*** *you who are seeking to be justified by law;* ***you have fallen from grace.***
>
> (Galatians 5:1-4)

Verse 4 is one of the most disturbing verses in the Bible: *"You have been severed...you have fallen from grace..."* Because it is not in Hebrews but Galatians, you can't use the same criteria to interpret it as what is used in Hebrews. The Galatians aren't under persecution, and they are most likely of a more international (Jew and Gentile) population. However, most importantly, they have not only mentally assented to Christ, but have received Him in their hearts as Savior. Therefore, this verse is most troubling because Paul is evidently speaking to a Christian running the risk of being severed from Christ! How can this be? My understanding of Scripture makes this an impossibility. It must be a mistake. A Christian severed from Christ?

Blasphemy

The only place where I can see this is possible is with the sin of blasphemy of the Holy Spirit. Jesus spoke of it in Matthew 12:30-32:

> *He who is not with Me is against Me; and he who does not gather with Me scatters.*
>
> *Therefore I say to you, any sin and blasphemy shall be forgiven me, but blasphemy against the spirit shall not be forgiven.*
>
> *And whoever shall speak a word against the Son of Man, it shall be forgiven him; but whoever shall speak against the Holy Spirit, it shall not be forgiven him, either in this age, or in the age to come.*

Jesus told of being unforgiven or unforgivable because of blasphemy. He was talking to a group of Pharisees who obstinately refused to receive Him, the answer to salvation and mankind's answer to sin, as Messiah. Not only do they refuse to receive Him, they actually infer that He's of Satan and continue to grasp at their answer to sin—the Old Testament answer of Law works and animal blood sacrifices.

This is very similar to the problem encountered in Hebrews 10:29 where the writer warns of the severe punishment of turning back to Law works and animal sacrifices. Doing so would:

- trample under foot the Son of God
- regard as unclean the blood of the covenant
- insult the Spirit of Grace

These cumulative truths speak of blasphemy of the Holy Spirit which is unpardonable. Blasphemy of the Holy Spirit consists of turning away from the precious blood of Christ, inclusive of insulting the Spirit of Grace and trampling the blood of the Son of God! This occurs, according to both Hebrews and Galatians, by turning back to Law works and to the ultimate insult of replacing Christ's precious blood sacrifice with the unclean and inferior blood of animals.

Only the sin of blasphemy could sever a believer from Christ. However, one could go back to a place that would bring such insult to the Spirit of Grace that it would constitute blasphemy and a severance from Christ—returning to the Law offering of animal blood after receiving the knowledge of the truth of Messiah and His flawless blood atonement.

A Grace Line

Could blasphemy be possible today? Come with me to a Law—Grace Line.(*see next page*)

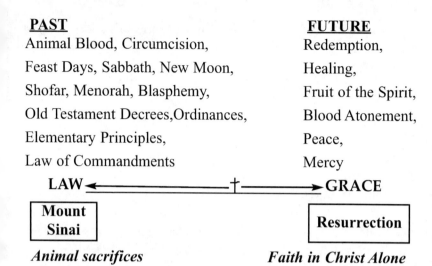

Note: Mt Sinai and Resurrection at the ends of the Grace Line

Along this Grace Line, starting at the cross, place legalistic external criteria that Judaizers say bring value to your relationship to Christ. Starting at the cross and working backwards on the line, I would take from the words of Colossians 2 and Ephesians 2, and list ordinances, Old Testament decrees, elementary principles, feast days, festivals, Sabbath, and ultimately back to circumcision, and animal blood sacrifices. On the line, moving forward from the cross, I would place new covenant promises such as grace, redemption, healing and ultimately the resurrection.

There is a great difference in embracing a feast day or a festival as it relates to your tradition and embracing it as it relates to your religion. If a Jew, or anyone else, cherishes tradition from his past because of national or even personal traditional value, it is certainly understandable. However, great error arises if these things are embraced as necessary for spiritual value and spiritual maturity.

What I embrace as tradition or endearing memories from my

past differs vastly from what I embrace as my salvation and my eternal life and destiny.

In Christ Alone

I hope that no one, not even the most eager legalist, goes back to offer animal sacrifices. Likewise, I hope that no one would entertain circumcision as a way to a deeper relationship with God. However, look at what this Grace v. Law exercise has accomplished. It has succeeded in turning you around, causing you to look back.

If Christ is salvation, if Christ is righteousness, if Christ is hope, rest, sabbath, faith, and future, then why *look back*? All of these external works take your eyes away from your proper direction, and serve only to turn you around. Your eyes and your attention move away from Jesus and back to things you will stumble over. If Christ is your focus, if Christ is your hope, if your righteousness and future is in Christ alone, then why even LOOK BACK, much less GO BACK?

Put yourself on the Grace Line at the cross and look back. What do you see at the far end of the line? Animal sacrifices. Why turn that way? Turn around. Turn toward God's great Sacrifice. Turn toward His grace and mercy and never turn back.

Why Go Back?

    Don't Go Back.

        Christ is better!

Remember These Key Points:

1. **Some Have Jewish Roots.**

    Jews have Jewish roots that relate them by blood to Moses, Abraham, Isaac, Joseph, David, and even Matthew, Mark, Paul and Peter. Their rich tradition and history is filled with great men and women of God and include other things such as the Torah, the Menorah, the temple, and the shofar. Furthermore, the Jews have the Holy Land!

2. **Others Have Coal Miner Roots.**

    Gentiles have Gentile roots. Mine are deep in the coal mining country of West Virginia where both my grandfathers worked. My father worked side by side with his father, deepening our family traditions.

3. **Nothing Remains the Same.**

    You really can't go back because nothing remains the same. You'll see that the house is gone, the store is gone, the corner station is a supermart, and the people have moved on.

4. **Level Ground Is at the Foot of the Cross.**

    The ground is level at the foot of the Cross. Christ leveled the ground and took away every advantage, except in Him. It doesn't matter how deep your roots or how shallow, because roots mean nothing! Only Christ means something. Christ means everything.

5. **The Great Exchange**

    You bring nothing to Christ, yet He gives you His everything. The Cross is the great exchange! At the cross, Christ took your

- darkness and gave you His light
- sin and gave you His righteousness
- disease and gave you His healing
- Hell and gave you His heaven
- death and gave you His life

6. **The Religion of Cain**

    You cannot add external works to your salvation to deepen your relationship with Christ. It doesn't matter what you do. What matters is who you are and whom you worship. Worship God, after all, you are His child.

7. **There Is Neither Jew Nor Gentile.**

    Flesh runs back to Law works because it loves the external criteria. The person in charge of the criteria becomes the judge, who gets to say who's in and who's out, who's holy and who's not, who's worthy, who's spiritual…the list goes on and on. For this reason, God doesn't allow that foolishness in the New Testament mentality. *Christ in you* provides the only hope of glory and the only avenue to spiritual maturity.

8. **Severed from Christ**

    *Y**ou have been severed** from Christ, you who are seeking to be justified by law; **you have fallen from grace.***

    (Galatians 5:4)

    Paul warned that a Christian can be severed from Christ. This can happen only if that Christian turns from the very thing that bought him in the first place—Christ's precious blood, and embraces the blasphemy of animal blood sacrifice.

9. **Blasphemy**

    Blasphemy of the Holy Spirit consists of turning away from the precious blood of Christ, thus insulting the Spirit of Grace, trampling the blood of the Son of God and turning back to the unclean and inferior blood of animals.

10. **A Grace Line**

    There is a great difference in embracing a feast day or a festival as it relates to your tradition and embracing it as it relates to your religion. Cherishing tradition from the past because of national or personal values is understandable. Great error arises if these are embraced as necessary for spiritual value and spiritual maturity.

11. **In Christ Alone**

    If Christ *is* salvation, righteousness, hope, rest, Sabbath, faith and future, then why look back? These external works turn your eyes away from the proper direction you should go. Don't go back—Christ is better.

Priceless Grace

I truly pray that you will understand the seriousness of what you have read in this book. Flesh works and carnal religion have a strong pull, even on the Christian. Sadly, much of the Christian church and, tragically, many preachers that fill its pulpits have not yet decided whether the church is a relevant new covenant ministry of life or a mixture of law, condemnation, grace, forgiveness, works, striving, and most any other confusing ingredient thrown into the mix. It's no wonder the New Testament church is so confused. It hears no clear call from the pulpit. Preachers feel like they must throw a little Law into the recipe to keep the people "living right."

Cheap Grace

Many preachers feel that if they preach too much "cheap grace" then Christians might just do anything. I think that some will stand before Christ one day and He'll ask what they mean by "cheap grace" because no such commodity exists.

While God offers grace freely, He did not secure it for us cheaply. Grace cost Heaven its very best. We receive it freely and should bow low everyday of our lives before the throne of God in thankfulness for this marvelous gift of God as we realize the great pardon and eternal promise bestowed upon us. It's free, but not cheap!

As it relates to the Law, grace may not seem fair, but grace doesn't relate to the Law. Grace relates to the heart and desire of God. Don't apologize for grace; receive it. God gave us this eternal theme and great gift in the New Testament, and we can only receive it and bow low in eternal thankfulness for it.

Those who don't think grace is fair will have to take that up with God. Paul didn't invent grace, God did. Christ brought us this wonderful gift of God and for the most part Paul revealed it as he wrote under the anointing of the Holy Spirit.

Christ came to make a difference. He didn't come to offer the old Law. If He had been satisfied with the old covenant law, He would have never stood up from the throne of God. However, the first testament fell short because man had no power to allow its success. Therefore, Christ came. He came to bring a New Testament, a new covenant different from the old, not of animal blood, but of God's blood, not of law, but of grace.

Is it different? Of course it is, and we celebrate that difference. This blood makes us free. It cleanses us once and for all and brings God's Holy Spirit to live God's desires in and through us from the inside out. God now writes His desires (His commandments) on our hearts and whispers His will into our Spirit ear. He comes in the Person of the Holy Spirit to live His will through us from the inside out.

> *And over all these virtues put on love, which binds them all together in perfect unity.*
>
> *Let the peace of Christ rule in your hearts, since as members of one body you were called to peace. And be thankful. Let the word of Christ dwell in you richly as you teach and admonish one another with all wisdom, and as you sing psalms, hymns and spiritual songs with gratitude in your hearts to God.*
>
> (Colossians 3:14-16 NIV)

Anyone still clinging to an external list of legalist rules is not only stuck in immaturity but is left behind in a cloud of grace dust. If you have to check your list to see what's right or what's wrong, then righteousness has passed you by. If you have to confer with your Ten Commandments or any other list of external criteria to see if you are allowed to stare at that scantily clad woman crossing the street, it's too late. By the time you've checked, you've sinned! The Holy Spirit lives in you and guides you into His continual righteousness.

Fear, condemnation, external legalism and holy trinkets aren't going to make a person "live right." Only the power of God's salvation overflowing out of a personal relationship with Christ will ever accomplish that. Remember that religion is man's vain attempt to reach and to please God. Salvation is God's successful and glorious attempt to reach man, and He has reached man through Jesus Christ.

God's Change Agents

Other factors exist in your relationship and growth in Christ other than His blood. Yes. It begins with and is released by the power of His blood and is enveloped in His blood, because nothing works without it. However, along with the power of His cleansing blood, God offers the power of the Holy Spirit and the power of the Word of God.

God uses many powerful change agents to bring you into Christian growth toward godly maturity. However, none of them are external religious paraphernalia that falsely promise to usher you into some deeper walk with God.

God introduces change agents to mature and shape us, drawing us into His presence. These Holy Spirit agents work on us internally, in our spirit, soul, mind, and attitudes. Christ comes to change our heart so He can change our mind. Christ comes to change our direction, our destiny, and our destination. He doesn't come so we can light candles and burn incense.

God's Word clearly tells us what results from the true change of

God's Spirit working within, through, and out of us:

> *But the fruit of the Spirit is love, joy, peace, patience, kindness, goodness, faithfulness,*
>
> *self-control; against such things there is no law.*
>
> *Now those who belong to Christ Jesus have crucified the flesh with its passions and desires.*
>
> *If we live by the Spirit, let us also walk by the Spirit.*
> (Galatians 5:22-25)

A Prayer with You

Thank you for reading my book. Remember that I love you and will be praying for you.

However, please remember, above all else, that Jesus loves you; He really does. God is not mad at you. His heart is driven to love you. Because of Christ alone you can stand totally forgiven through His great gift at Calvary.

If you don't know Jesus Christ personally, please receive this message: Receive Christ as your Savior today. Too many will miss Heaven who know *about* Christ, but have never *received* Him as Personal Savior. Romans Ten, Nine & Ten, is the TNT of the Bible:

> *That if you confess with your mouth Jesus as Lord, and believe in your heart that God raised Him from the dead, you shall be saved;*
>
> *for with the heart man believes, resulting in righteousness, and with the mouth he confesses, resulting in salvation.*

That's the Gospel. Believe Christ and receive Christ. With your heart you believe, and with your mouth you confess. Repeat this prayer after me. God is listening; Heaven is paying attention.

> *Father, God. In the name of Jesus, I confess that I believe the truth of Your Gospel, the Good News of eternal life through the Savior, Jesus Christ. I confess my sins to You, Jesus, and believe Your promise to forgive me of my sins and cleanse me with Your Blood. Come into my heart. Sit on the throne of my life. I give my life to You. I believe You and receive You as my personal Savior. Thank You for receiving me and forgiving me. In Jesus' Name, Amen.*

That really happened just then. It is not related to how you feel, and what just happened to you is not based upon your emotions. It is based upon the Solid Rock of God's promise. You are not a Christian because you are worthy. You are a Christian because Christ is Worthy. Spend your life, from now on worshiping Him and following Him. Jesus, your very best Friend, will never leave you nor forsake you.

Tell a friend what Christ has done for you. Tell them that you have accepted Jesus as your personal savior. Contact me; I have a good Bible for you, and I will help you find a great church.

I celebrate with you in your new life. You are now a new creation in Christ Jesus. And remember, *Christ is Better—Don't Go Back!*

Larry Linkous is a third generation preacher, born and raised in a ministry home. A deep love for Christ and a passion for the lost fostered in that environment drew Larry into the ministry at the early age of 21. After fifteen years of ministry through radio and in the pulpit, Larry and his wife Sandra founded New Life Christian Fellowship in 1983. Larry is the Senior Pastor of New Life in Titusville, Florida, a multiracial, interdenominational church that is continually experiencing tremendous growth in both membership and maturity. Pastor Linkous leads a staff of 12 pastors who help serve this multi-thousand member congregation.

In 1990, Larry began a daily radio program called "Thee Morning Drive," which airs live each weekday morning. This two hour morning drive program is now syndicated to many stations throughout the nation and has become the "spiritual breakfast" of many thousands of listeners throughout the country. He also serves as President of Daystar Public Radio Inc. with radio station interests throughout Florida.

Whether on radio or television, from his pulpit or pulpits across the nation and the world, Pastor Linkous is busy creating vacancies in hell by compelling the lost to Christ and bringing heaven to earth by challenging Christians to embrace their God-born destiny. Out of that same passion, Larry brings the powerful message of this book that will challenge and possibly even change your life.

For more information on Pastor Linkous' books and tapes, you may contact:

New Life Christian Fellowship

(321) 269-7578

Web Site: *www.findnewlife.com*